BASKETRY *of*
the APPALACHIAN
MOUNTAINS

BASKETRY of the APPALACHIAN MOUNTAINS

Sue H. Stephenson

VNR VAN NOSTRAND REINHOLD COMPANY
New York Cincinnati Toronto London Melbourne

To John, Graham, and Taft

Copyright © 1977 by Van Nostrand Reinhold Company Inc.
Library of Congress Catalog Card Number 76-40095
ISBN 0-442-27972-8

Printed in the United States of America
Designed by Loudan Enterprises

Published in 1977 by Van Nostrand Reinhold Company Inc.
135 West 50th Street, New York, N.Y. 10020

Van Nostrand Reinhold Australia Pty. Ltd.
480 Latrobe Street
Melbourne, Victoria 3000, Australia

Van Nostrand Reinhold Company Ltd.
Molly Millars Lane
Wokingham, Berkshire, RG11 2PY London

Macmillan of Canada
Division of Gape Publishing Limited
164 Commander Boulevard
Agincourt, Ontario M1S 3C7, Canada

16 15 14 13 12 11 10

Library of Congress Cataloging in Publication Data
Stephenson, Sue H.
   Basketry of the Appalachian Mountains.
   Bibliography: p.
   Includes index.
   1. Basket making.   2. Basketwork—Appalachian
region.   I. Title
TT879.B3S74   746.4'1   76-40095
ISBN 0-442-27972-8

Photographs by Aubrey Wiley, Lynchburg, Virginia

Note: Dates of the baskets and places of origin, where there
is reasonable certainty, are given in the captions of the
photographs. Unless otherwise noted, all splint baskets are
made of white oak. The directions for making the baskets shown in the photographs begin on the page numbers
given in the captions in parentheses following the description of the basket

Drawings by Anne Warner and Lyndon Whitmore

Frontispiece: Twin-bottomed egg basket, the ''master piece''
of splint basketry. (Page 65.)

Contents

Acknowledgments

My first acknowledgment must be to another book on basketry, one of the best instruction manuals on wickerwork that I have encountered. My progress on this book has been hastened at every step by the information contained in *Baskets and Basketry* by Dorothy Wright (David and Charles: Newton Abbot, England, 1974).

My special thanks go to my photographer, Mr. Aubrey M. Wiley, Jr., and to three students at Randolph-Macon Woman's College—Anne Warner and Lyndon Whitmore for their drawings and Emily Freeman for her research assistance during her junior year at the University of Reading, England.

To the many helpful and imaginative librarians, both in the United States and in Scotland, England, and Germany, and to the many, many people in the Appalachian Mountains who took the time to search their memories (and their attics) for the lore of the baskets and the brooms, I am deeply grateful.

I should like, particularly, to express my appreciation to the following people in Europe for their unfailingly gracious and extensive assistance: Mrs. G. M. Pot-van Regteren Altena in Holland; Mr. Alfred Schneider, the director of the Staatliche Fachschule für Korbflechterei in Lichtenfels, West Germany; Miss Dorothy Wright, Mrs. F. E. Lanchester, and our cousin, Mr. T. R. Stephenson, in England.

Not all of the many individuals who contributed baskets for study can be listed here, but I would like to mention a few who gave me free access to outstanding collections: Mrs. G. M. Alexander, Mrs. Max Guggenheimer, and Mrs. John Early Jackson of Lynchburg, Virginia; Mrs. Violet Edwards of Danville, Virginia; Mr. and Mrs. David Nash and Miss Rachel Nash of Alderson, West Virginia. (I am further indebted to Mr. Nash for his assistance in developing the tool for use in the oak-rod basket.)

It is not always that an author has the opportunity to express gratitude *and* affection, at the same time, to a primary source. I was very fortunate: my grandmother, Mrs. Ada Burns Scott, was an invaluable part of this book.

Finally, my deepest appreciation is reserved for my husband who, with great good nature, felled oak trees, disentangled himself from miles of honeysuckle vines, and, in general, aided and abetted this project in every way.

Preface

When I was a child, living with my grandparents in the southern mountains of West Virginia, my grandfather said to me one day, "When you grow up, I want you to *remember* these beautiful old hills." It was to me then, as it is now, a very moving and poignant request.

This book, in many ways, is an expression of gratitude for my heritage from the Appalachian Mountains—a few tributary acorns rendered unto the Oak.

My background in the mountains begins in 1769 with an Ulster-Scot from the Shenandoah Valley who settled his family on the Greenbrier River in what is now West Virginia, and who thereupon proceeded to fight, in one way or another, for the remainder of his life. First, there were the Indian raids in the Greenbrier Valley near Lewisburg; then came the Revolution; and after that, more Indians. He spent a full eight years fighting to secure the release of a seven-year-old daughter captured by an Indian raiding party. He succeeded in his efforts, I am happy to say. His massive three-story home of hewn logs is still standing at Lowell, West Virginia, and, like the druidic Celts of another time, it pleases me that it is built of oak timbers.

My mountain heritage ends with a grandmother who is now in her hundredth year and who is still knitting socks on #1 needles.

A vigorous clan they were, and I am grateful to them for many things, but especially for the pleasure of creative handcraft that they very carefully developed in me as a child.

During World War II, I was sent to live with my grandparents, three of whom lived in the same mountain village on the New River in Summers County, just over a mountain from Lowell.

One grandfather was a farmer and orchardist. He pronounced the word "either" as "ither," with a short i, and he was the determined keeper of a vast store of knowledge concerning plant life, ghosts, and the processing and refining of a liquid beverage venerated by generations of other forebears who also pronounced English words in a characteristic and idiomatic way. It was, he felt, absolutely none of the Federal Government's business how he practiced his birthright on his own land. He was a truculent citizen of the United States, who suffered fools poorly.

My other grandfather, together with one of his sons, more or less ran the village. They owned the "downtown," all but the railroad and its depot in the middle of things. They ran the sawmill, the large general store, stuffed with everything from horse collars to groceries, the feed store, the one-pump filling station, the garage that had once been the livery stable, and a fleet of trucks that my grandfather used for his timber business.

The village of Sandstone contained perhaps fifty families. The total area of it was not much beyond a hundred acres, but it served as a transportation center for several remote mountain areas.

I mention all of this to make the point that when I was by my grandfather's side, I was literally at the hub of a very isolated, very rich, and even today, little understood cultural unit. In the summertime I went "timbering" with him. We went throughout the mountains, an old man and a little girl dressed in bib overalls, asking a question a minute. (City children have much to learn.) I remember that we carried tin lunch pails and walking sticks to guard against snakes. Fortunately, the people of the mountains enjoy children's questions; in fact, they are born teachers. What was especially important to me was that the people we encountered allowed me to participate in any activity that interested me, from stirring apple butter to cutting out dovetail joints.

I sat on benches and nail kegs on store porches, listened to mountain "yarns," and learned how to whittle with my grandfather's penknife. Some of the woodsmen who worked for him taught me how to make whistles, other toys, and baskets.

The hallmarks of a self-reliant culture are excellence and versatility in manual skills. I consider that my grandmother was unusually skilled; moreover, she had an innate sensitivity to and taste in color and design. She taught me needlecraft—everything from spinning to embroidery.

In some respects, it was the last chance to learn at first hand the old ways of "doing and making do." The war with its scarcities forced people to return to their earlier folkways that were, even then, dying out. My grandmother, born in the mountains in 1877, knew the technology of everything from soap making to the lost art of drying and sulfuring apples and the dessication of vegetables and other fruits to preserve their maximum flavor. As a child in a sugarless world, I was grateful for her skill with honey and maple syrup.

In retrospect, I believe that my rather intensive education in the four or five years that I spent with them was closer to that of the early 1900s than to the 1940s elsewhere. For one thing, my grandparents were then in their sixties and seventies and they were consciously passing on their traditions to an only grandchild.

The Southern Highlanders, as the Appalachian settlers have been called, have an affinity for handcraft by nature as well as nurture. The urge to master things is well-developed in our characters. I would even go so far as to say that it is a genetic trait. (The relatively small genetic pool was reduced further by the tendency of the Scottish settlers to marry their own cousins. There are two first-cousin marriages in successive generations in my own family.)

Whatever else the culture of the Appalachian Mountains has become in the past two hundred years, it is still distinctive, stubbornly Anglo-Saxon, or Celtic, to be more exact, and conservative. This has a bearing on almost all of our crafts, as we shall see later with the baskets.

Apart from the obvious necessity of crafts in the mountains, there is another environmental factor that tends to keep handcraft viable there. It is little realized by those outside the mountains how *physically* close a mountain child is to raw wood and plant fibers.

We were engulfed by wood products. Wood is one of the world's best toys. Slab wood and tree trunks are lying about everywhere. A playhouse and all of its furnishings can be constructed by post and lintel in an hour. The materials for seesaws, crude sleds and wagons, slingshots, any simple machine a child's mind can devise, are rarely more than a few yards away in the mountains. Rocks, too. We loved to build with stone and wood scraps and to furnish our "homes" with grass mats and vine baskets. I made my first "Nine Patch" quilt at the age of ten for a doll's bed in a handmade playhouse.

My own urban sons are surrounded by plastics—not so malleable a material as wood for a child, and, I think, not so much fun.

It is because my grandparents wished me "to remember" and because I want my sons "to know" that I have done the research for this book. I hope that a moribund craft can be preserved before its technology has entirely disappeared.

Most of the research for this book has been confined to the valleys and passageways through the Blue Ridge and the Allegheny Mountains to the Greenbrier Valley—from the Shenandoah Valley in Virginia to the eastern counties of West Virginia. These are the routes traveled by the earliest settlers. It is an area less well known than the North Carolina and Tennessee Smokies.

Because of the revival of handcrafts in the Smoky Mountains during the early part of the twentieth century, and their subsequent commercialization, it is often difficult to locate early basket models outside of museums. A great deal of the basketry of North Carolina and Tennessee has now been alloyed with that of the Cherokee Indians, techniques of the cloth weavers, and outside commercial influences.

In contrast, the remoteness of such places as the Goshen Pass in Virginia, or Keeney's Knob in West Virginia, has isolated original specimens, some in a remarkable state of preservation and many with a long family provenance.

Basketry, particularly splint basketry, is a difficult craft. This is one of the reasons for its demise. By way of illustration, I went to see a blacksmith from North Carolina about making a small froe for me. "What on God's earth do ye want a *froe* fur?" he asked. When I told him that I was making splint baskets, he observed, "Well, Sister, you have surely picked yourself a craft *there*!"

It takes fifty hours to make a twin-bottomed egg basket. The weaving is extraordinarily simple, but the shaping and molding of the oak requires hand skill of a high order. The best approach is a careful, yet easy, concern for each step of the process; eventually, a basket will emerge and, without doubt, it will outlast your lifetime.

The Terminology

"If you tell somebody today that you're lookin' for a froe, they're liable to think you got a speech defect . . . like a three-year-old tryin' to say 'throw.' I bet you any amount of money, nine out of ten people won't know what you're talkin' about."

Antique dealer from Virginia

Nine out of ten people do *not* know what a froe is. I have placed this glossary of unfamiliar terminology at the beginning of the book with good reason. The reader is requested to read the list of terms before proceeding to the main text of the book.

Awl A pointed tool, similar to an ice pick, used for making holes in willow rods and for opening spaces in the weaving.

Bastard Cut A with-grain cut in wood along lines that are tangent to the growth rings of the tree (Fig. 1-1).

Board Cut A cross-grain cut in wood along radial lines of the tree (Fig. 1-1).

Bool A circular rim.

Border In wickerwork, the interweaving of the basket spokes around the upper rim of the basket to lock the weavers in place.

Brake A wedging device, or clamp, to hold the log in place while it is being split.

Butt The thicker base of willow or other rods. The upper end is known as the "tip."

By-Stake An extra stake inserted beside an upright foundation stake.

Coiling A method of basketry which involves the wrapping and sewing together of loose, bundled materials arranged in spiral coils.

Foot An extra border woven around the outside edge of the basket base for protection of the basket bottom and for added strength.

French Slew Diagonal randing weave. (See Fig. 5-4.)

Froe A cutting tool consisting of a long metal blade with a handle attached at a right angle on one end to provide leverage (Fig. 1-2).

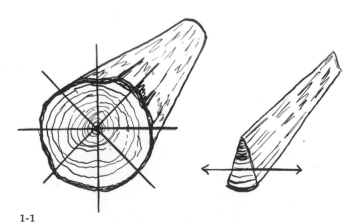

1-1

1-2

Glut A wedge-shaped piece of wood used for splitting logs (Fig. 1-3).

Osier A willow rod.

Pairing Weave A weaving pattern consisting of two strands alternately twisted over each other around each stake. (See Fig. 5-6.)

Plaiting The interweaving of flat basketry materials (Figs. 1-4, 1-5).

Randing The over and under weaving pattern consisting of a single weaver woven alternately in front of one stake and behind the next. (See Fig. 5-1.)

Rib A rod or a splint inserted into the weaving to serve as a foundation element.

Rive To cleave or split.

Scarf Joint A type of joining made by trimming the stock from one inner edge and one outer edge of the ends of a rod or a splint in order to create one piece of a continuous thickness. (See Fig. 4-8.)

Slath The arrangement of crossed stakes in the base of the basket that makes up the initial foundation. (See Figs. 5-17–5-19.)

Slew Randing weave with two or more weavers. (See Fig. 5-3).

Slype A slantwise cut. To make such a slicing, angled cut (Fig. 1-6).

Stakes or Spokes Used interchangeably. The vertical (usually) members of the framework of the basket.

Upsett The turning up of the spokes of the basket sides at the bottom edge of the base. Also, the several rounds of special weaving that serve to reinforce the upturned spokes.

Wale A weaving pattern consisting of working three, four, or more rods in succession over a varying number of spokes and behind one. (Waling is more often called "coiling" in American terminology; however, this is a misleading term.) (See Figs. 5-7–5-9.)

Weavers The flexible, horizontal elements of a basket.

Wickerwork Round rod weaving over a firm framework.

Withe A willow rod. A slender shoot of any tree.

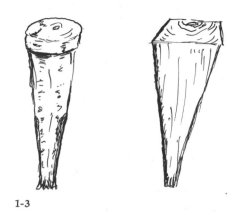

1-3

1-4

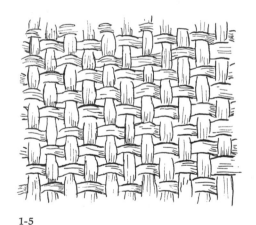

1-5

1-6

The Baskets —
Their Uses and Origins

"You know that song, 'A tisket, a tasket—a green and yellow basket?' Well, I used to sing that when I was little, so my daddy, he got Mrs. Gwinn to make me a wee little egg basket ... She pulled the tiny little splits through the weavin' with a crochet hook, Mama said. Well, Daddy painted the basket yellow, and Mama wove a little green ribbon around the rim, and they put one egg in it on a nest of grass and that was my Easter basket. It was the cutest present I ever got in my life, but our homeplace burned down several years ago and the basket was in it."

A young woman from West Virginia

Basketry was a major implement in the daily lives of the people of the Appalachian Mountains. Together with cloth sacks, wooden barrels and boxes, baskets made up the total sum of a settler's devices for storage and for transporting what could not be contained in his hands.

Although there is a considerable amount of overlapping in usage, the mountain baskets fall into four main categories: (1) storage containers, (2) heavy baskets for agriculture, (3) measurement containers, and (4) house baskets.

STORAGE CONTAINERS

While grains were usually stored in wooden bins in a dry outbuilding, apples, potatoes, and other root crops were stored in root cellars dug under the house. Large, coarse baskets of splints, and especially willow, or wickerwork baskets made from rods of other hardwoods, were used to separate these crops.

When such crops were not actually buried in the ground and covered with layers of earth and straw, as frequently they were, they had to be culled from time to time to remove decaying pieces. The farmer went through each bas-

ket of apples, for example, transferred the good ones to another basket, carried the rotting ones out of the cellar to empty, rinsed his basket, and allowed it to dry in the air. Cone-shaped willow baskets were ideal for such storage. They cradled the fruit gently, allowed it to "breathe," and they dried out rapidly. Willow had an affinity for mildew, but so did everything else in a root cellar. (There is a pungent odor that is specific for old log cabins. I call it "eau de apple." Like wood smoke, it permeates everything. In examining old wickerwork baskets and the sievelike apple-drying baskets, I always smell them for the lingering, musty odor of the apple.)

Willow baskets are the most rare of all the surviving Appalachian baskets. The craft nearly died out completely in the last half of the nineteenth century. One reason for this was the lack of suitable material. There are some fifteen to twenty species of willow, both trees and shrubs, growing in the mountains, but the ideal basket willow—long-stemmed withes with leaves growing at the tips of the rods—required cultivation and regular pruning. Wild willow is difficult to work with; it is lacking in "kindness," as the English basketmakers call it.

There are two small areas in West Virginia today in which a species of basket willow (*Salix purpurea*) is growing. It is assumed that this willow, native to Europe, has escaped to the wild from a site of former cultivation.

An article in the March, 1835, edition of *The Cultivator*, (later, *The Country Gentleman*), published in Albany, New York, urges the farmer to cultivate a patch of basket willow with which to make "many useful baskets" on cold winter evenings. Residents of both central

1. Top left: market basket. Right: storage basket made of unpeeled maple rods, c. 1860. The twisted rope border on the basket identifies it as a continental European style, probably German or Dutch. This type of border was not a traditional English style. Bottom: a gathering basket.

and western Virginia subscribed to this periodical. Willow, nevertheless, was eclipsed by white oak splints and wickerwork made from other materials.

I have found shoots of dogwood, elm, maple, and poplar woven into extremely heavy storage baskets. In the area around Alleghany and Bath Counties in Virginia, I found three wickerwork baskets woven of blackberry canes. These were small "house baskets" and, as a class, belong with the honeysuckle baskets. I suspect, however, that larger baskets of this material once existed in that area.

If it were not for the presence of so much wickerware in materials other than willow, which is the ideal material for this type of basketry, the inference might be drawn that flat-plaited splintwork was the only basketry known in the mountains. Included in this chapter are several photographs of old wickerwork baskets in willow from The Museum of English Rural Life at the University of Reading, England. Compare these baskets from Scotland, England, and Wales with their stylistic counterparts from the Appalachian Mountains on page 60. The change of material from willow to white oak is almost the only difference apparent in the ribbed baskets. Even the names of the baskets are the same.

The basket shown in Plates 35 and 36 (page 90) dates before 1850. It could easily be mis-

taken for an European willow basket of 1800—until it is lifted. It is an extremely heavy basket made of white oak rods, each carved to resemble an osier. The elements are 50" long and about ⅛" in diameter. The basket, in perfect condition, originated near Salisbury, North Carolina. It has been in constant use in one family since the late 1840s.

I have encountered several other copies of "willowware" made of carved hardwood rods, all of them scattered through the Shenandoah Valley. In technique and in form, the baskets are German.

It is evident that in nearly all of the ribbed splint baskets an attempt has been made to create *rounded* elements for the framework of the baskets. In this sense, the ribbed splint baskets are actually a variety of wickerwork made with oak splints. Since splints are naturally flat, flat plaiting would have been the weaving technique least demanding of time and energy. One must assume, therefore, that the mountain basketmakers were copying a pre-existing style. From the evidence offered by the traditional baskets from the British Isles, that style was round-rod wickerwork made of willow.

There was also, in northern England and Scotland, a long tradition of flat-plaited splintwork, believed to have been brought to England by the Scandinavian invaders. Splint baskets, made from copse-grown oak rived with the identical tools and technology in use in the Appalachians, are still being made in Lancashire, England.

AGRICULTURAL BASKETS

The second category of mountain basketry is the utilitarian carrying basket. Perhaps 95 percent of these are splint baskets. They include all of the rectangular gathering baskets, the well-known ribbed "egg basket" (also called a "hip basket" from the fact that when it is carried in the crook of the elbow, a part of its weight rests on the hip), the "hen basket" that later assumed the function of a woman's handbag, and all of the cylindrical and rectangular "field baskets."

With the exception of the "field baskets," all of these were clearly designed for carrying weight over long distances, either on foot or mule and horseback. They have a low center of gravity, heavy, rounded handles that fit the hand, and they are well balanced. Round baskets in the shape of a truncated cone were not used for heavy loads because the wide diameter of the top shifts the load too far from the vertical line of the shoulder. Large round baskets were usually cylindrical in form and they were often used with shoulder yokes in older days. I remember that shoulder yokes were considered very archaic and "old fashioned" in my grandparents' day.

2. Left to right: one-and-a-half-bushel basket, c. 1850; berry basket, c. 1850; rectangular house basket, early 1900s.

The "hen basket" shown in Plate 30 (page 60) (called by Allen H. Eaton in his book, *Handicrafts of the Southern Highlands*, the "Carolina Basket," apparently for want of another descriptive name) has an ancient lineage. According to Dorothy Wright, in *Baskets and Basketry*, this basket is known in Scotland as an "Ose basket," or the "Skye hen basket," from the island of Skye where they are regularly made. Some writers have suggested that its origins are in Scandinavia, but according to Dorothy Wright, "in Sweden, the basket is known as 'The Scotch Basket.'"

This basket in recent history was used in Scotland to carry broody hens from one farm to another in the days before incubators. Its function in the Appalachian Mountains in my grandmother's time was to confine a hen that was being carried to market. Gradually, it came to be used as a shopping basket and, still later, as a woman's handbag. My grandmother tells an amusing story about one of these baskets. She had a neighbor who had once let one of her young infants slip out of the back of a willow shopping basket that she was carrying over her arm during a six-mile walk to the store. Before her next child was born, she had a large hen basket made and from then on transported her infants in perfect safety.

3. Left to right: egg basket, hickory market basket; berry basket, c. 1875.

4. Traditional Welsh potato basket. (Photograph by courtesy of the Museum of English Rural Life.)

5. Traditional hen basket from Scotland. (Photograph by courtesy of the Museum of English Rural Life.)

The best-known basket of the Appalachian Mountains remains the ribbed "egg basket." Its framework is composed of two intersecting bools, or circular rims, and a number of spaced ribs. The weaving locks all of these elements together in a strongly woven texture.

There are many variations on the ribbed basket, some of them rectangular, but the prototype appears to be the rounded egg basket. It is also a basket that defies printed directions because of the many variables in its structure. It can only be made with experience and common sense.

The curvilinear basket, as used in the mountains, is ideal for transporting eggs. The twin bottom and the curved sides hold eggs in place perfectly. Egg baskets are made in many sizes and are still in use today on farms in the mountains for gathering eggs.

Because the egg baskets represented something of a tour de force of the basketmaker's skill, they were frequently made in miniature and given as gifts to children, or presented as clever containers holding tiny gifts for women.

Field baskets are just what the name implies. Usually made of white oak splints, they were large one- and two-bushel baskets used for gathering agricultural produce. Most of them are cylindrical in form and some have heavier splints added to the bases to protect the bottoms as they were dragged along from row to row in the fields. The potato basket, Plate 30, used in the mountains, is identical in form to that of northern England and Scotland, Plate 4.

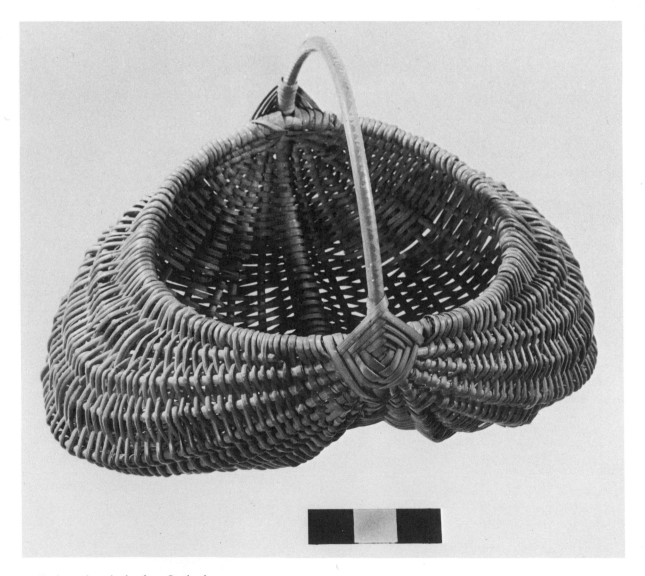

6. Traditional egg basket from Scotland.

7. Miniature egg basket, c. 1890, on left. A "four-dozen" egg basket, right, c. 1915.

8. Rectangular ribbed market basket, c. 1900. Greenbrier County, West Virginia. This style of basket, with its sharp corner angles, is probably a late-nineteenth-century innovation of the Appalachian basketmakers. It is a hybrid style, combining the appearance of the rectangular flat-plaited splint baskets with the traditional round-cornered rectangular baskets in rib work that were the older forms. The prototype of this basket may be seen in Plate 16. It is strictly a white-oak basket: no other wood will bear the stress of the sharp bends, and usually even this type of basket shows splintered fibers at the corners of the ribs.

9. Eight-inch-square ribbed basket, c. 1910. Pocahontas County, West Virginia.

10. Large field basket illustrating base "shoes," c. 1880. Greenbrier County, West Virginia.

11. Left to right—Top: square-bottomed apple basket,
c. 1860. Rectangular basket with "shoes" on base. Handles
not original. Bottom: half-bushel egg basket, c. 1885.
Crude willow basket. The handle on this basket is a master-
piece of confusion; nonetheless, it is surprisingly sturdy.

MEASUREMENT BASKETS

Because barter was the principal medium of economic trade in the mountains, measurement was highly important. Storekeepers maintained barrels and small tubs provided by coopers for exact measure, but the customer used bushel and peck baskets. Some basketmakers in the Shenandoah Valley used wooden forms, carved from tree trunks, to make cylindrical measuring baskets of uniform size. Basketmakers farther west in the mountains seem to have taken a disparaging view of the use of any kind of form or mold. More often, a farmer simply "sized" a new basket by pouring in a known quantity of grain or other material and marking the level on the inside of the basket. Many larger baskets can be found with these marks still present.

The difficulty of maintaining measurement standards can be seen even today in the widely varying standards in different states for bushels of heaped measure. The Bureau of Standards was not established until 1901, but in 1856 a set of weights and measures employing the Winchester Bushel was sent from England to the United States. The Winchester Bushel, a cylinder measuring 18½" in diameter and 8" high on the interior and containing 2150.42 cubic inches, is the standard bushel in use today in the United States.

In Pocahontas County, West Virginia, an elderly man pointed out a large basket in his grain shed as being an "old bushel basket." The basket being of a larger size than a bushel, I started to look for the bushel mark when he said, "That's one of them old Scotch bushels; the Scotch people around here used a bigger bushel sometimes." The only explanation that I can find for his remark is that there was a measure called a "firlot," equal to one and one-half times the Winchester Bushel, which was used in Scotland as a measure for oats and barley.

HOUSE BASKETS

A wonderful supply of house baskets exists today in mountain homes, the ravages of antique dealers notwithstanding. They survive as treasured heirlooms. These are the baskets used, for the most part, by the women in the family. They include the round, oval, and rectangular rib baskets, rectangular market baskets, hen baskets, sewing baskets, wool-storage baskets with lids, nests of round "service" baskets, berry-picking baskets, the "two-pie" or "church-social" baskets, and the large, flat Victorian baskets, or what my grandmother calls a "provender basket."

Another small basket, the finely woven "key basket," turns up every now and then, always with an interesting family story to it. Key baskets were used by the mistress of a plantation to hold the various keys to storage rooms and buildings under her control. The key basket hung on the wall of the lady's workroom in the "mansion house." Rectangular key baskets found their way into the mountains either by way of later settlers who left their plantations in Virginia after the Civil War, or by inheritance. A few were undoubtedly used by the eighteenth-century settlers who established the same large plantations in the mountain valleys, but, as a rule, they are "imported." In any case, they survive as a symbol of an ancestress's status in life. Key baskets made in the mountains show the persistence of the ribbed style; they are in the form of half an egg basket (Plate 14).

All of the above are woven of splints. A variety of baskets exists in other materials.

12. Hickory key basket, originally from Georgia. 5" × 8".

13. Key basket, originally from Amherst County, Virginia.

14. Mountain key basket. Bath County, Virginia.

15. Left: square-bottomed apple basket. Monroe County, West Virginia. Right: flat-bottomed egg basket. Summers County, West Virginia.

16. Traditional ribbed willow basket from the British Isles. (Photograph by courtesy of the Museum of English Rural Life.) Baskets made in this style, along with the hen basket, the egg basket, and the round service basket, are the oldest baskets of the European immigrants in the United States. They continue to be made today in the Appalachians with little alteration in their original forms other than a change in material from willow to wooden splints.

Opposite:
17. Left to right—Top: melon-shaped egg basket, dyed dark brown; market basket (page 55) . Bottom: round basket with a square handle; blackberry-cane house basket.

18. Clockwise from top left (on chairback): "gray splints," c. 1850. Pittsylvania County, Virginia. Unpeeled willow basket after the style of the Madeira baskets. A bushel egg basket. Gathering basket. Large dough basket of coiled rye straw bound with split blackberry cane (page 98). Dough basket of wheat straw bound with white-oak splints. Egg basket, c. 1860. Henry County, Virginia. Dark brown melon basket (on chair seat).

One quite early basket is the "dough basket," used for the rising of bread dough. It is made of spiral coils of wheat, oat, or rye straw and bound either with thin splint or strips of bark from other plants. Dough baskets were made in Pennsylvania and in the Shenandoah Valley among the German settlers, who also made beehives of coiled straw. (Bees were unknown in this part of the mountains before the arrival of the white settlers. The Indians called the honeybee "the white man's fly."*) Dough baskets were used also in the eastern parts of Maryland and Virginia during the Colonial era. The craft of coiled straw was widespread throughout western Europe. It is still an ongoing craft in Scandinavia, certain areas of Germany, Wales, the northwest of Britain, and the western islands of Scotland. These baskets appear to have been the only baskets of the coiling technique that were a native craft among the white settlers of the Appalachians. Coiled baskets made of pine straw from the southern long-leaf pine (*Pinus palustris*), a southern tree whose range is limited to the southern end of the Appalachians, owe more to the Indian culture in that area than to the European tradition.

*Oren F. Morton, *A History of Rockbridge County* (Staunton, Virginia, 1920), p. 37.

Without going into the probable European origins of the splint basketry of the Cherokee Indians in the mountains of North Carolina, it is well known that the design and technique of the coiled basketry of the American Indians is without equal anywhere. Considering the broad exposure of the early white settlers to the Indians of many different tribes, the fact that the settlers made no attempt to adopt either design or technique from the Indian basketry is merely another instance of the persistent hostility of these settlers to anything "foreign" to their own culture. It is not, I feel, an oversimplification to state that this attitude of the people of the Southern Highlands is a salient feature of the entire culture. My grandparents, for example, gently ridiculed my "city accent" when I went to live with them, and my fellow students at school not-so-gently chased me home from the third grade with rocks until I was able to alter my speech patterns to their liking. I have personally had hundreds of opportunities to observe the irony attendant upon a meeting between a stranger to the mountains and a mountain native—each displaying a faintly patronizing attitude toward the other and neither of them fully aware of it.

There is ample evidence in the internal construction of wickerwork baskets to show that, before the turn of the twentieth century, the basketry traditions of the Indians and the European settlers were divergent.

19. Dough basket made of corn fodder and bound with white-oak splint. Greenbrier County, West Virginia.

The typical wickerwork basket bases used by Indians in the East are illustrated in Figs. 2-1–2-3. Basket bases of the mountain whites show that of the usual European arrangement of spokes in Figs. 5-18 and 5-20 (see Plate 20).

Indians do not care much for the common "pairing weave" (Fig. 5-6) of the mountaineers. When they *do* use it, the top weaver of the two is nearly always twisted to the left, or counterclockwise, instead of the European clockwise twist. An even number of spokes, woven by means of the two-strand "chasing" technique, is typical for Indian baskets (Fig. 5-2).

Color and patterned weaving as used by Indians were rarely used by the mountain basketmakers before the craft revival in the Smokies. Other than the "gray splints" basket (Plate 27, page 52) and a few splint baskets dyed with walnut hulls, which I know to be prior to 1850, I have not encountered another early mountain basket that showed any evidence of having been dyed.

The Indian methods of splitting willow (using the teeth and both hands) and obtaining splints from logs is completely different from the woodworking traditions of the British Isles. (Indian basketmakers "waterlog" their trees, then pound the bark until single splints can be stripped free of the pole.)

20. European-style basket base. (Photograph by courtesy of the Museum of English Rural Life.)

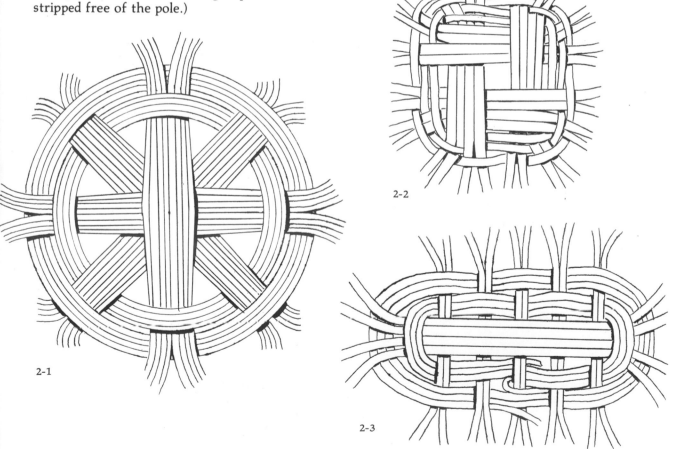

2-1

2-2

2-3

Finally, the shape of the baskets and any decoration used in their surfaces seem to be based, in Indian work, upon symmetry of line. Proportioned *areas* are characteristic for the baskets of the mountain whites; that is, areas of different sizes in the baskets will often be found to be related to one another in the same proportion.

"FOREIGN" BASKETS

The Shenandoah Valley during the late eighteenth and nineteenth centuries was the great highway between the ridges of the Blue Ridge and the Alleghenies. Not only settlers traveled it in the early part of the century, but also, by 1840, itinerant peddlers were crisscrossing it making side trips into the surrounding mountains. A well-known route traveled by tinsmiths and gypsies after the Civil War led from the Shenandoah Valley to the Greenbrier Valley, through the Kanawha Valley and into the Ohio Valley. Many of these peddlers sold baskets of various origins. Nineteenth-century European willow basketry arrived in the mountains in this way. The baskets have the look of the professional basketmaker: there is a variety of different weaves in each basket, borders are more intricate, and nearly all of the wickerwork baskets have superior handles and reinforced foot borders.

They were immediately copied in honeysuckle, native willow, and many other materials by the basketmakers living near the "sophisticated" high road. Rockbridge County, Virginia, was particularly rich in these basket copies; however, these basket styles made little headway in the high mountains to the west until the time of the revival of basketry in the Great Smoky Mountains in the twentieth century.

The professionally made willow baskets in the mountains fall into two separate groups. Before the Civil War, we find an older style of basketry from England, Germany, and Holland—doubtless, most of it brought into the area by immigrants. The baskets sold by early itinerant peddlers seem to have been made in New England and Philadelphia.

21. Left: willow hamper, c. 1895. Germany. Right: willow basket made of both peeled and unpeeled withes, c. 1850. Of German or Dutch origin.

Shortly after the Civil War, there suddenly appears an influx of excellent European basketry, made in a wide variety of styles and willow material.

It is difficult to trace the origins of these late-nineteenth-century European baskets. Basketry, in Europe, reached a high peak of popularity and commercial success between 1850 and 1900. Ordinarily, craftsmen in basketry tend to repeat, ad infinitum, the styles common to their geographical areas. Indeed, basketmakers' guilds jealously protected their own wares. Until 1808, in Holland, no basketry outside the local guilds could enter the territory except on the day of the Yearmarkets, or trade fairs. This was a common European practice.

Beginning sometime before the middle of the nineteenth century, basketmakers began to copy the basketry of other regions with great avidity. Basket styles spread rapidly. Many styles were taken over intact, while others suffered modifications to suit the makers. At the same time, experimentation with different varieties of basket willow occurred, in spite of rigid importation laws on plants. *Salix Americana*, a popular type of willow among Dutch and German makers, was smuggled into Europe in the following ingenious way. A basketmaker made a basket of green rods, carried it on board ship with him, and carefully watered it daily in his cabin. Upon reaching his destination in Europe, he took the basket apart and used the rods as cuttings.*

In 1893, Lichtenfels, Germany, the greatest basketmaking center in the world, exported $192,000 worth of basketry to the United States. By 1895, this willow basketry was filtering into the Appalachians.**

The baskets in Plate 34 (page 89) are key objects in the study of the dissemination of basketry traditions. The style is at least as old as that of the seventeenth century in Spain.

In the paintings of several seventeenth-century Spanish painters, notably Francisco de Zurbarán (1598–1664), are some astonishing baskets. Both the splint baskets and the willow baskets might easily be mistaken for baskets found in the Appalachian Mountains in the twentieth century.

English basketmakers call the braided borders on these willow baskets "Madeira borders." They might have been introduced into England around 1807 when the British occupied Madeira for some seven years.

I have not been able to date their appearance in the Appalachians before 1880. After that time, they are ubiquitous in certain areas. Crude as well as expert copies of the baskets exist in willow, honeysuckle, and such vines as Virginia creeper. Indian basketmakers have copied them frequently, using the runners at the base of the coralberry plant (*Symphoricarpos orbiculatus*).

At least three routes of travel to this country are known. Early in the nineteenth century, sea captains brought them home from the islands of the Portuguese Azores. Also, the baskets were a part of the German-made basketry imported at the end of the century, the style having spread from southern Europe into Germany. Perhaps the most interesting source of the baskets led, via a circuitous route, to gypsies.

In the early part of this century, gypsies were a frequent sight in the Appalachians. They camped in the laurel thickets in the mountains, made rustic furniture, fern stands, and the like from the native rhododendron and willow, and then sold this ware in the nearby towns. In the sixteenth and seventeenth centuries, both Spain and Portugal shipped gypsies to their colonies in South America. They are said to have gradually worked their way through Central America and Mexico, entering the United States in the 1860s and 1870s. Probably because of the Civil War in the East, they do not appear in the Appalachians until 1875–80. That they made this style of basket is certain. There are many people in the mountains who remember watching them at work.

Basket weaves are obviously simple enough to have been invented simultaneously in many cultures, but again and again it has been shown that subtle differences exist among all peoples in their preferences for the expression of esthetic form and design. A single basket bears a cultural signature whether it has been copied or not. When a splint basket made by a Scotch-Irish settler is placed next to the same style of basket made by a member of the Cherokee Indian tribe in the mountains of North Carolina, the difference is apparent to the trained eye. The detail in the basket made by an Indian weaver will nearly always be more tightly controlled than that of the mountain white.

*Christoph Will, *Flechtwaren* (Bamberg, Germany, n.d.).

**Sir. J. L. Green, *The Rural Industries of England* (London, 1895), p. 166.

22. Top: oval splint basket, c. 1910. Bottom, left to right: oval willow basket, late nineteenth century. Small copy of Madeira-style basket in honeysuckle, Alleghany County, Virginia. Copy of Madeira-style basket in willow.

THE BASKETMAKERS

Who were the basketmakers of the Appalachians? According to my grandmother, almost every family knew something of the skill—certainly, splint making was a common woodcraft skill that a nineteenth-century boy acquired as he was learning his axecraft. Even as late as the 1940s, boys were still learning to cut shingles and to build rude farm shelters with no more than an axe. Carpentry, for a mountain boy, always began with felling the tree, just as sewing, for my grandmother, began with harvesting flax and shearing the sheep.

Basketry at one time was nothing more than a common household skill—not at all in the class with cooperage, for example—possibly because it required so few tools and, for a culture accustomed to a wide variety of hand skills, it was relatively a simple craft. Many of the baskets are crudely wrought "homemade" affairs.

At exactly what time basketry in the mountains became a medium of commercial exchange, being a partial or even a principal means of livelihood for certain families, is not known. It is known that by the 1870s baskets were being sold or traded to grocery stores. At one time in West Virginia the exchange rate was a bushel of corn for a bushel basket, or a one-pound loaf of sugar for a two-peck basket.

By the early part of the twentieth century, basketry was "butter, egg, and basket money" for housewives, and many women took up the craft.

Folklorists might be interested in the evidence of surviving remnants of the basketmaker's terminology in the speech of the area:

Osiers. Willow shoots are not called "willow shoots" in the mountains; they are "osiers."

Sallow or *Sally.* (*Salix?*) Another term for willow.

Withe. A slender rod of any tree. My grandmother's favorite paddle, or "switch," was "a withe from the cherry tree." In England, a withe, or withy, refers specifically to the osier.

Slype. Slype is a transitive verb meaning to slice to a point. "Slype the end of the wooden glut on both sides with an axe." The term is used by English basket workers to mean an angled cut at the end of a willow rod. A slyped cut allows the woven round rod to present a flat surface on the basket sides.

Spelk. Another term for a splint. "Granddaddy wove that lath fence with white oak spelks, cut board fashion, and pegged into chestnut posts." Oak splint baskets in England today are known, also, as "spelk" baskets.

Swill, Slops. In the mountains, both of these words referred to food for swine, usually leftover vegetable parings and other scraps. In northern England, where splint baskets are still being made, the baskets themselves are called "swills" and "slops."

Preparation of the Materials

"I wish to the Lord someone would figure out a way of makin' baskets out of that ol' Kudzu vine; hit's about to cover up Asheville!"

A North Carolina woman

SPLINTS

A splint, or "split," is a flexible, thin strip of wood cut from the annular rings of white oak (*Quercus alba*), hickory, maple, white or black ash, and, occasionally, from hazel, elm, or poplar.

Of these woods, white oak was preferred to all others by the mountain basketmakers, with hickory in second place. Hickory, slightly more dense than oak and very springy, makes excellent rims and handles. It is more difficult to split into thin strips than oak, but I have discovered that it splits with more ease if the pole is rived into billets as soon as it is cut and then seasoned for a month before removing the splints. Additionally, while both woods will become brittle over the years if they are not immersed in water from time to time, thin white oak splints will lose their resilience more slowly than hickory. The average life of a well-made splint housebasket, assuming it receives some moisture every now and then, is fifty to seventy-five years. Many, of course, are far older.

The usable part of the tree is the base—from about 6" above the ground to the first projecting limb or indication of a knot. The log should be 5" to 6" in diameter and from six to ten feet in length. (Maple and elm should be no larger than 4" in diameter.) It must be completely straight, with no evidence of twisting in the scales of the bark. It should have no scars or projecting twigs larger than a pencil. Twigs form knotholes that extend from the heartwood through the grain of the wood, making removal

of the splints from that area of the log additionally frustrating.

The perfect white oak is nearly always found to be growing in mature forests on the north side of mountain slopes. Its struggle for light induces it to grow straight up, and it does not waste its energy putting out side shoots until it reaches a safe height.

Sometimes the wood in a particular tree will be found to be rather stringy or spongy in appearance. There is no way of knowing in advance whether a tree will be of firm fiber. Drooping limbs are said to be an indicator of an inferior tree, but the best log I ever split had sagging limbs. I look for a tree standing somewhat apart from other oaks, growing in rich, loamy soil. The worst tree I ever encountered was growing in a clay soil.

The log, now called a "pole," should be rived within three or four days of cutting for best results, but it may rest for as long as five months, if necessary.

Obtaining the splints is the most tedious part of making a basket. The skill takes a little time to master, and one's maiden effort can result in a collection of splinters and very short splints (from which *small* baskets can be made). It is possible to reduce a pole to twenty-five pounds of neat, clean splints with no more than a poll axe, one stick of wood for a wedge, another to use as a mallet, and a penknife. I prefer, however, to apply every useful tool known to have been employed in the craft to make this physically difficult task easier.

I make use of leverage wherever possible. For this, a froe and some kind of wedging brake are indispensable. To the best of my knowledge, froes are no longer being manufactured in this country. Antique shops specializing in country tools often have them, or a machine shop can make one from a piece of strap iron. The metal should be at least ¼ inch thick, the *dull* blade about 12 inches long, and the handle about 20 inches long. The crotch of a large fallen tree will serve as a brake. I have, at times, propped the pole against an outside staircase, taken a position on the stairs, and moved down the steps as the froe descended through the length of the pole. Wedging the end of the pole by some means other than standing with one's feet in the split means better leverage and greater control over the opening split.

All cuts throughout the splitting process are made from the top of the pole toward the base.

First, examine the growth rings radiating from a central point across the top of the pole. Not all trees are symmetrical. Place the froe directly across the diameter of these rings in order to bisect them. Tap the froe into the wood with a mallet. Seesaw the froe into the pole by striking the protruding end of the froe and pushing downward on the handle end. As soon as the froe is imbedded in the end of the pole some nine or ten inches, lay the pole on the ground, step on the lower edge of the split, lift the handle of the froe, and insert a wooden glut just below the cutting edge of the froe. Properly made, a glut is a carefully smoothed wedge of seasoned hardwood—the very hardest, such as dogwood, persimmon, or ironwood beech. In the absence of these, a wedge-shaped piece of oak, cut with an axe, will serve this purpose very well. Two gluts will be needed. (Steel wedges can be used, but they tend to bruise and to splinter the wood unnecessarily.)

After the first glut is in place, remove the froe, turn the pole on its side, and drive in the glut until the split has opened enough to receive the second glut. Continue in this fashion, glut over glut, until the entire pole splits into two equal halves. The initial division of the pole is the most difficult.

Again, examine the growth rings at the top and bisect each half, this time using only the froe as a lever. It is at this point that a brake becomes useful. If, for any reason, the wood is unyielding, the gluts will have to be used again. There are now four sections of the pole, or "billets," as they are termed. Each of these is divided, making a total of eight billets.

Now begins the actual riving of the with-grain, "bastard cut" splints. Pick up one of the billets and examine the top. The heartwood can be distinguished from the sapwood by color; it is clearly darker. Place a small froe, or a hunting knife, in the growth ring channel that separates the two colors. Tap in the blade gently about 5" and open the split with leverage until there is space for the fingers of both hands. Wedging the billet between the knees, pull apart the two sections, gradually working the hands down the length of the billet (Fig. 3-1). If the wood binds at any point, use a knife or the froe to free it.

Ordinarily, the heartwood will split off cleanly from the sapwood, but from this point onward in the splitting process, great tactile skill is called for. The splitting wood has a tendency to run out toward the outer edges of the billet. The rule is that the split will run toward a curve and toward a thin side. It is often possible to *feel* the beginning of a "runout" before it can be seen: there will be a slight pressure shift. When this happens, stop immediately and examine the lines of the annular rings along the sides of the billet and also the fibers inside the split. After determining the direction of the runout, pull down the opposite, or thicker, piece and give it a sharp jerk to bring it back into line (Fig. 3-2). As the splits become thinner, this procedure should be done more slowly, using the fingers and wrists more than the arm muscles.

Reserve all of the heartwood for future handles and rims and save the bark for dye-stuff (to be discussed later).

Take up the sapwood piece and skin off the bark with a penknife or the drawknife (Fig. 3-3). The sapwood section, by this time, will be a fairly flat strip of wood some two or three inches thick. Find the middle channel in the thickness which will serve to bisect the strip. Brace the strip between the knees or under an arm and work a penknife into the channel until enough space has opened to admit the thumbs of both hands. (A safety tip: keep the index finger on the top of the knife blade. In this way, if the knife slips, the index finger will hit the top of the wood and the knife is prevented from slicing into the lower hand holding the strip.) Pull apart gently, using equal pressure on both sides. Keep the thumbs close to the split all the way down to the base (Fig. 3-4).

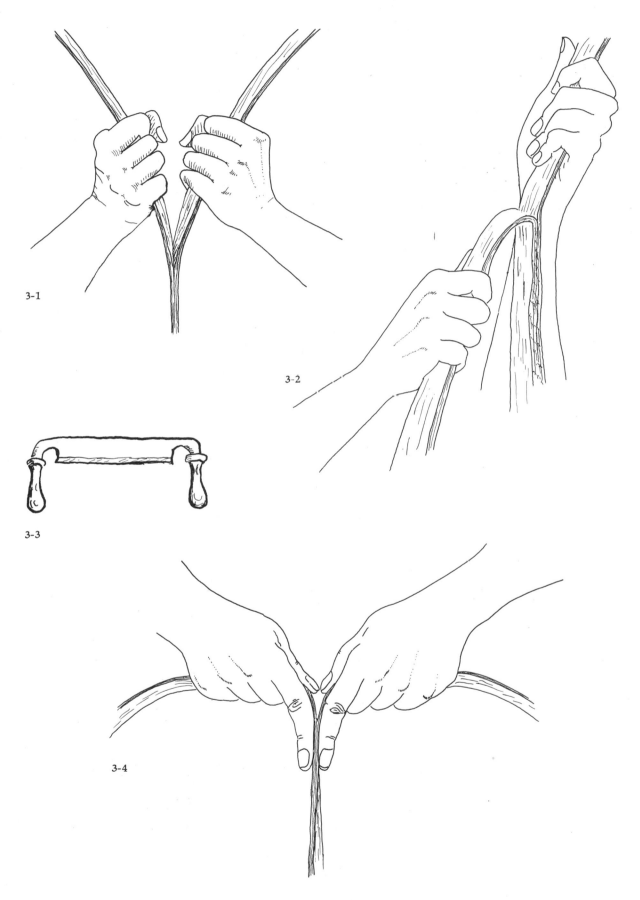

3-1

3-2

3-3

3-4

Continue to divide each section of the strip by halves until the splints are reduced to the thinness of a single annular ring. Do not attempt to split off a single, thin piece from a thicker section; always halve the sections. It will be obvious, by this time, that a split need not follow exactly the channel of the growth ring and that, if the rings are wide, this thickness can be split, too.

As each billet is finished, place the splints in a shaving horse and dress them with a *sharp* drawknife until they are of uniform thickness (about 1/16" to ⅛") and satin smooth. Trimming for width will be done later when the baskets are woven. A plan for the construction of a shaving horse is given in Fig. 3-5.

The drawknife method is by far the easiest way to smooth the splints. The knack of using the tool is quite simple. Block planes are useless on green wood; a spokeshave, if it is very sharp and kept clean of shavings, will work *slightly* better; nothing, however, can compare with the usefulness of the drawknife for this type of planing.

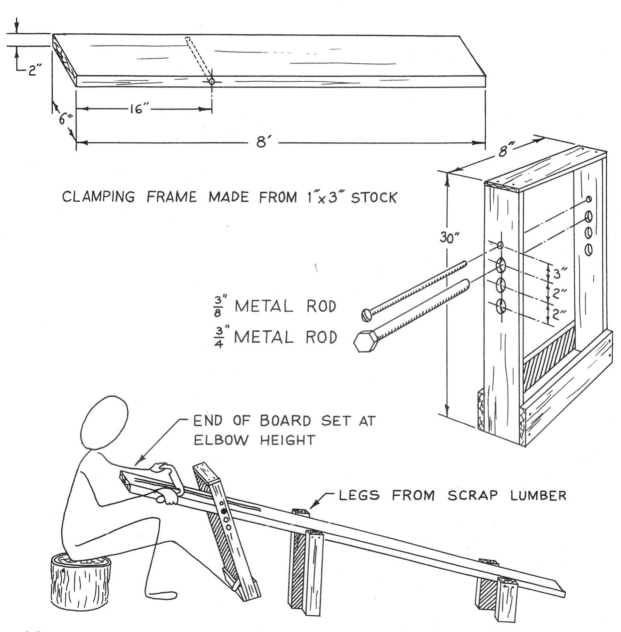

CLAMPING FRAME MADE FROM 1"x3" STOCK

$\frac{3}{8}$" METAL ROD

$\frac{3}{4}$" METAL ROD

END OF BOARD SET AT ELBOW HEIGHT

LEGS FROM SCRAP LUMBER

3-5

Another technique for smoothing fine weaving splints must be learned as well (Fig. 3-6). Put a piece of leather over a knee. Place a rough splint on the leather and clamp it against the knee with a sharp penknife. Hold the blade perpendicular to the splint and press it down with the index finger. Pull the splint against the knife blade with the other hand. Plane the splint in this fashion until it is completely smooth and free from thick, hard places.

The splints should be grouped by length and bundled together. Store them in a dry room to prevent mildew discoloration; they will keep indefinitely. All that is required is a ten-minute soak in tepid water before using.

It is a good idea to leave a few double-thickness splints to use for reinforcement strips and the inside rim pieces. The heartwood sections can be split into ½" and ¾"-thick pieces from which handles and rims will be carved later. These should be bastard cut, too.

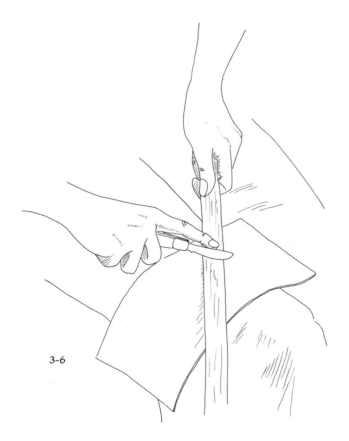

3-6

WILLOW

A singular feature of willow is its need for water. (A mature willow tree will drink forty gallons of water a day.) Willow rods not only have to be well soaked to begin with, but they must be kept continuously damp while they are being worked. A small peeled withe will dry out to the breaking point in fifteen minutes.

In lieu of true basket willow which is difficult to locate in the United States, weeping willow (*Salix babylonica*) will serve as the nearest substitute.

Select at least one hundred withes from four to six feet in length for a medium-sized basket. Some will break. Coil them gently to fit inside a large tub or kettle and boil them for six hours. Osiers gathered in spring, when the sap has risen and just before they break into leaf, do not need to be boiled. Peel them by rubbing off the bark with a coarse towel; place the wet withes immediately in damp newspapers or a large plastic lawn bag to "mellow" for twenty-four hours. Use damp willows within three or four days; they will mildew quickly. (The rods will be more pliable if, after peeling, they are seasoned for at least three months.)

Dry, seasoned withes, depending upon their size and whether or not they have been peeled, will need to soak from thirty minutes to three days and a mellowing period of at least twelve hours. If it seems that some larger rods are still too brittle to bend, place them in rapidly boiling water for fifteen to thirty minutes. Some experimentation with the material is necessary.

Admittedly, "wild" willow is a difficult material. The shoots are less uniform in size than basket willow, short twigs and leaves must be removed, and their tensile strength is highly variable from tree to tree and shrub to shrub; nevertheless, once the weaving has been completed, these baskets are amazingly strong and lightweight.

Osiers can be split lengthwise with a penknife to make flat weavers, called "skeins." Some of the interior pith will need to be planed off. This is done in the manner of smoothing splints—by pulling the withe against a penknife held on the knee.

HONEYSUCKLE

Although honeysuckle and other vines have been used in European basketry for a very long time, it would appear that this particular vine became a substitute for willow in the mountains. It is a splendid material, easy to work with because of its long runners that are considerably more flexible than willow. Its natural peeled color is a pale greenish white that will bleach in the sun to white. It darkens with age to a pale tan color. Basketmakers in the mountains often soaked honeysuckle baskets in an infusion of tea to produce the buff tan color of willow. It takes careful examination of old baskets to distinguish the two materials. They were frequently used together in the same basket, the willow being used for the base spokes and heavy handle foundations and the honeysuckle for weavers.

There are several varieties of honeysuckle (family *Caprifoliaceae*) that are native to the mountains. These have a fairly solid pith. (Asian imports do not.) By now, there are both native and imported honeysuckles, many of them hybridized, all over the United States. The best type will have a solid pith and it will have long, straight runners. If the vine has a chance to climb on anything, it will twist itself into unusable coils; therefore, look for that which is growing flat on highway embankments, hanging down from cliffs, or growing in open fields. It forms dense mats in these areas.

Loosen a handful of the vines and slowly trace one of them to a source root. Either cut it or tear it loose. Keep the butts of the vines together in one hand until a roll of about two inches has been collected; then make a coil of the vines, leaves and all, measuring about a foot in diameter. Sew the ends of the vines in and around the coil to keep it from unfurling. Two medium-sized baskets can be made from three or four of the coils, provided the runners average six to eight feet in length. The vines can be collected at any time of the year, but autumn will see the longest vines.

Stuff the coils into a large kettle of water, place a lid or a flat rock on top of them to keep them submerged, and boil the vines for three hours. Remove one large coil at a time, unroll it and, working with one or two vines, rub off the bark and the leaves by passing the vines through a rough towel or a *plastic* pan scourer held in one hand. The vines then can be lightly cleaned in soapy water with a brush but it is not absolutely necessary to do so. Rinse them well. Select four vines of uniform thickness and re-coil them. Allow the small coils to dry in the sun.

Hang them in a dry room until ready for use. Before using, soak them in tepid water for twenty minutes.

Honeysuckle will absorb any kind of dye readily. Water-based dyes or stains are recommended.

PREPARATION OF MISCELLANEOUS MATERIALS

BLACKBERRY OR RASPBERRY CANES

These materials have the advantage of uniform thickness and a natural mahogany color. Select the canes at the end of their growing season, in October. Use heavy work gloves and pruning shears to cut the canes about 6″ above the ground. Starting at the tips, *push* the thorns off the canes with one gloved hand while pulling the rod through the palm with the other hand. Snap off stubborn thorns with a push sideways. Do not use a knife if you wish to preserve the color. If the canes are still "green," they can often be worked in this state; submerge the occasional stiff cane in boiling water for five to ten minutes.

If the canes are dormant and brittle, follow the instructions given for honeysuckle. Soak well in tepid water before using.

HARDWOOD RODS

Straight one-year shoots of dogwood, mulberry, elm, hazel, sassafras, and sugar and red maple are excellent materials for wickerwork baskets, but they are extremely heavy and difficult to weave from the standpoint of physical strength. They are usually woven unpeeled and in a green condition. Maple, sassafras, and mulberry seem to spring up overnight in old fields in the Appalachians. The slender shoots are easily gathered with pruning shears. They should be about ¼″ to ½″ in diameter at the butts and at least three feet long.

When willow is unavailable, maple twigs are a useful substitute for the larger stakes needed for basket bases when weaving with honeysuckle. Slight curves can be straightened with moist heat, but it is best to ignore twisted or knotty woods.

The mountain basketmakers were eclectic in their choice of woods. Actually, any hardwood at hand can be used provided it meets the requirements of size, strength, and pliability.

To recapitulate: in order to peel the bark of dormant plants, or to increase pliability, boil (or steam) the materials in water for a length of time varying with the species. Unless the material contains natural moisture from its own sap, it will have to be well soaked in tepid water before using.

COILED STRAW

Coiled straw baskets are simple to make and the materials for them are among the easiest to obtain.

There are two traditional tools used in this craft that are not so easy to find. The first is a bone awl made from a rear leg bone of an old horse. (There are times when even the vast resources of the Appalachian Mountains fail me: I must confess that I have been unable to locate the hind leg bone of *any* horse, old or young.) The second tool is a straight section of cow horn.*

The tools probably will have to be improvised. I use the handle of a tortoise-shell mustard spoon for the awl. The principle to be observed is that the awl, used for opening up spaces in the tightly packed straw to receive the flexible binder, must be strong, blunt-tipped, and smoothly polished so that the delicate straw will not be damaged. Polished bone will slide

3-7

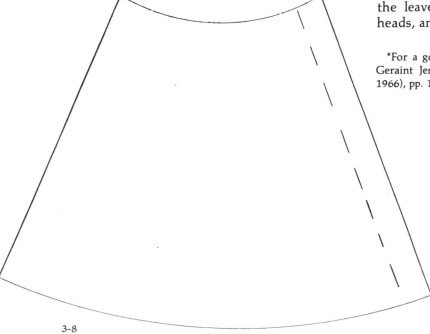

3-8

through the straws without tearing them. Both plastic and wood will break easily. A 6" scrap of ivory, ground down to the proper size and polished, is ideal. The awl should be a thin, flat strip about ⅜" wide with a narrow blunt tip at one end.

The funnel-like section of cow horn is used for shaping the coils of straw. New straws are inserted into the *center* of the bundle through the back of the horn. The forward opening in the horn measures from ½" to 1" in diameter. The horn remains in position, a few inches ahead of the binding, throughout the making of the basket (Fig. 3-7).

Figure 3-8 shows a pattern for making a "horn" from a piece of tin or heavy leather. The diameter at the top is ¾". Reduce or expand the pattern as desired.

The soft sheen of pale gold wheat or oat straw, bound with the red-mahogany bark of raspberry or blackberry canes, is unexcelled in loveliness. These are the traditional materials of this basket. It requires more skill to use wheat straw because of the short lengths, but such a basket is well worth the effort.

Winter-grown old-fashioned bearded wheat, long-stemmed and hollow, is the type required. The wheat must be cut close to the ground with a sickle, about a week before it would normally be harvested. (The lower stems will have some green color still showing.)

Spread the bundles of wheat on an old blanket to dry in the sun for three or four days, turning the straw each day. Remove the wheat to a dry, covered area at night. When it has dried, remove the leaves, tie it in bundles around the seed heads, and hang in a dry area.

*For a good description of the craft of strawwork, see Geraint Jenkins, *Traditional Country Craftsmen* (New York, 1966), pp. 136-48.

Before using, stack it in small groups and cut off the seed heads. Soak the straw for twenty minutes in water, wrap it in a damp towel to mellow for another thirty minutes.

Rye straw, a brassy gold color with a high gloss, has longer, tougher stems than wheat, so it is easier to work with. Prepare it according to the directions given above for wheat.

Many other grasses and plant fibers can be used for coiled baskets. It is fun to experiment with both materials and colors. (Flattened oat straw, woven over ¼" dyed splints, makes charming miniature baskets. This combination was, in fact, one of the earliest baskets that I made as a child. I colored the tiny splints with a brown crayon. Simple, miniature baskets are good exercises for teaching the craft to children.)

BINDING MATERIAL

Thin splint is used frequently. There are many other barks that combine strength with greater flexibility: raspberry and blackberry canes, willow, leatherwood, poplar, and slender vines. The inner bark of hickory, cedar, hemlock, and poplar can be peeled from the inside of the rough outer bark of these logs.

In all cases with outer barks, the bark is skinned from first- or second-year shoots. Use a penknife to make parallel cuts down the length of the bark. Tap the bark all over with a padded mallet, pry up the edges of the piece in several places, and peel the strip gently from the pole. If the strips are gathered in the spring as the sap is rising through the cambium layer of the tree, this operation is quite easy.

Since raspberry and blackberry bramble need an annual pruning, it is a simple economy to make use of this beautiful and strong material at that time. My preference is raspberry for both its color and its ease of working. The canes are stripped of briars as described on page 36. Use a sharp penknife to divide each cane into four pieces, starting at the tip and working toward the butt. The knack of splitting the canes is easily acquired. It is not unlike splitting an oak pole with a froe—merely scaled down in strength.

Keep the blade of the knife centered in the rod; use it as a lever from time to time to open the split. Seesaw the blade in tight spots, and watch for "runouts."

Clamp each quarter of the rod upside down on the knee and pull it against the perpendicular blade of the knife to scrape off the interior pith.

The canes and other barks are best worked "green." They will remain pliable for several hours. If they dry out, soak them in water.

23. Contemporary miniatures. Top to bottom: honeysuckle. Base formed over a penny. Honeysuckle woven over hickory splints, 2" diameter. Honeysuckle woven over split Norfolk reed (*Phragmites communis*). Norfolk reed, used as roof-thatching material in England, grows wild in the mountains, usually in undrained bogs.

Splintwork

"Our daddy used to tell us, whenever we was children learnin' to do a new kind of skill, 'It's just like makin' a split basket: ain't no shape a'tall to the first one or two you make, but the third one is the easiest thing on earth.'"

A West Virginia farmer

GENERAL RULES FOR SPLINTWORK

Let the tool become an extension of the hand. Learn to "feel" with the cutting edge of the tool. A tactile sense will be developed quickly if you continue to concentrate on this awareness of the edge of the tool.

Following are some tips on measuring and marking:

Always use a flexible tapemeasure.

The use of a large piece of ⅝" fiber board or soft pine, with a squared grid marked off at ½" intervals, is an invaluable aid to lining up stakes for rectangular basket bases. (The other side of the board can be marked with concentric circles, bisected in eighths, for round bases.) Spokes can be taped down with masking tape or pinned to the board with drawing pins to hold the stake ends in position for the beginning of the weaving.

The easiest way to maintain the shape of the sides of a rectangular basket is to use the board in the following way: after the base is woven and the side stakes have been scored and bent upwards, drive four 10d or 12d finishing nails into the board at the *outside* intersections of the four corners. The side weavers can be pulled tautly around the four nails for the first several rounds of weaving, after which the nails are pulled out of the board (Fig. 4-1).

Dimensions of basket stakes should include at least a 2" allowance on each end for the "tucking in" at the top border.

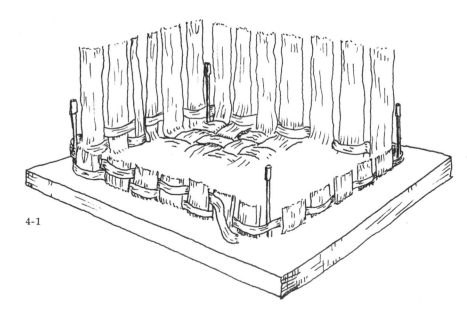

4-1

Rectangular baskets with a single handle should have an uneven number of stakes on the two long sides to permit the handle to be centered. Splint baskets are more often woven in spiral fashion over an uneven number of stakes. The uneven number is created by splitting one stake, rather than by the insertion of an extra one, as is the case in wickerwork. Twill weave (see Fig. 1-4), woven spirally, also requires an uneven number of stakes.

In joining a new weaver, first measure and cut off the end of the old weaver flush with a stake. Overlap the old end with the new through two or four of the same stakes. Be certain that both ends are concealed behind a stake (see Fig. 4-2).

The formulas for obtaining the volumes of the most common forms of measurement baskets are given here:

4 pecks = 1 bushel = 2,150.42 cubic inches = 35.24 liters.

Volume of a rectangular solid = L (length) × W (width) × H (height).

Volume of a cylinder = $\pi r^2 \times H$ (π = 3.14159).

Volume of the frustrum of a cone = $\frac{1}{3} H\pi (r^2 + R^2 + Rr)$; H = slant height; r = radius of the base circle; R = radius of the top circle.

SOAKING AND TRIMMING THE SPLINTS

Soak the splints in tepid water for ten to twenty minutes. Check them for even thickness and shave high spots, if necessary. Trim the damp splints to the desired width with a *good* pair of sharp scissors, such as a heavy pair of good sewing shears. (Splints used green, from a just-rived pole, may be trimmed and used without soaking.)

When the directions call for splitting a stake in a round base, use the scissors and a straight cut. Stake splitting on the side of a rectangular basket is done in the following way: drill a ⅛″ hole at the base of the splint; split the stake from the end to the hole and then trim some of the stock from both edges of the split with a penknife until the split is as wide as the diameter of the hole. This will ease the passage of the weaver through the split.

Basket stakes should be about ⅛″ to 1/16″ thick in the average basket, with the weavers about 1/16″ to 1/32″. Stakes should *always* be thicker than weavers. Widths of stakes and weavers vary with the size and use of the basket. Proportion them accordingly.

The topmost weaver in the basket should be trimmed at a gradual slope for several inches to allow it to meet the spiral without creating an abrupt, uneven step in height.

Always allow a freshly woven basket to dry out for at least forty-eight hours before completing the top border. The splints will invariably shrink in the drying process and the weaving will become loose. (Wood shrinks crossgrain.) After drying the basket, pack the weavers down on the stakes until they are tight; then add additional rows of weaving as needed.

4-2

BENDING THE STAKES

Stakes should be well soaked. Score the stake on the inside of the bend with a dull knife. A slight crushing of the fibers is all that is necessary. Use your fingers to maintain contact with both sides of the crease. Force the stake slowly, but firmly, upward. Some of the stakes may splinter slightly; ignore this unless there is a complete break. (Unusual.) If a stake should break, trim it neatly, select a new splint with more tensile strength, trim it to size and insert it well into the weaving beneath the broken stake. Bend up the new stake and continue.

After the basket sides have been completed and dried, every other protruding stake will be thinned with a penknife and tucked *over* the last row and down through the weaving to the inside of the basket. The procedure is as follows: Turn the basket upside down and soak the stakes for ten to twenty minutes. Score the alternate stakes. Fold over the stakes and mark the ends to lodge behind the third or fourth weaver from the top. Cut the ends to a shallow point. Use an awl or a narrow screwdriver to open up the weaving and force the stakes down beneath the inside weavers. Cut off the alternate standing stakes so that they will be flush with the top of the basket (Fig. 4-3). If, for any reason, the basket is not to have a rim, do not cut the standing stakes, but instead fold them over and push them down through the weavers on the outside of the basket.

HANDLES AND RIMS FOR SPLINT BASKETS

The handle is one of the most important elements in the entire basket, from the point of view of both design and engineering. The single handle is the basket's balancing point, from which most of the weight is suspended. A well-made basket, by definition, must have a well-made handle and one that is firmly attached to it. Splints may dry out and break, there may even be holes in the bottom of the basket, but the handle must remain intact.

Because the shape of the handle completes the design line of the basket, its size and configuration should be considered from the outset in making a basket.

Most mountain carrying baskets have wide, thick handles and wide rims (or a rim and a dowel) to match them. These handles fit the hand; they give a feeling of stability and comfortable security to the baskets. The thick (¼" or more) handle serves as a suspension spring: walking provides the compression, or "bounce," while the spring of the handle relieves the arm of some of the work of carrying a dead weight. This is one of the reasons that the more elastic hickory was preferred for heavy handles. The close-grained heartwood of a tree is the wood of choice for handles and rims.

4-3

The general procedure for making a curved handle will serve to illustrate most of the techniques involved with handles. The particular handle strip, some ¼" to ⅜" thick and about 1" wide, is clamped in the shaving horse and planed on both sides to an even thickness with the drawknife. Mark the allowances for insertion into the basket sides on each end of the strip and plane these to a lesser thickness. Make an even chamfer cut along the outside edges of the *underneath* side of the handle (Fig. 4-4). Remove the strip from the shaving horse.

Hold the strip against a knee and use a sharp penknife to smooth the chamfers until they are rounded (Fig. 4-5). Taper the allowances on the ends to a point that is about ¼" wide (Fig. 4-6). To whittle a tapered point, make a series of slicing cuts beginning at the tip and work backward in stepwise fashion; then smooth the edges. The handle is now ready to be bent into its curved shape.

Provided the heartwood has been split recently from the pole, it will be green enough to bend into shape without soaking. Simply wrap the entire length around a straight tree trunk that is 7" or 8" in diameter. Hold it in place for a minute or two; the curve will retain the arc while the ends are being attached to the basket.

If the handle has been made from seasoned wood, it will have to be soaked in hot water (or steamed) for thirty minutes or boiled in water for fifteen to twenty minutes. It then should be pliable enough to bend without any splintering.

There are several ways of attaching handles. Field baskets nearly always have handles with notches cut to support the rim. Many of the carrying baskets show notched handles, too. Most old baskets reveal handles that were inserted through the weaving on the sides, through and across the basket bottoms, often with an extra reinforcement splint slipped in over the join on the bottom. Perhaps the best method of handle attachment, as attested to by the survival of old baskets with still secure handles, is illustrated in Fig. 4-7 .

The end of the handle is trimmed (and thinned) to a point, inserted through all side weavers and brought out at the basket's bottom edge. Here, the splint is resplit, bastard fashion, with the penknife. The lower half is worked over the first weaver of the base and through all the others to the center base. (The illustration does not show the entire length of the splint: carry it through to the center of the base.) The top half of the splint is folded back over one side weaver and worked upward

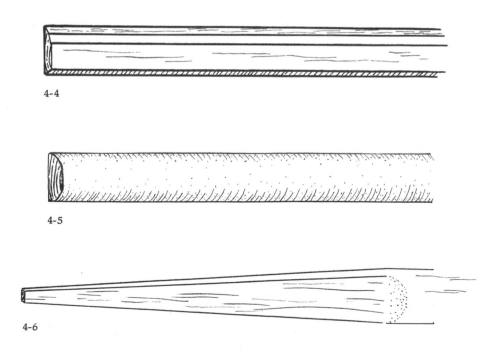

4-4

4-5

4-6

through several side weavers, its point being concealed beneath a weaver. (The handle may, or may not, be pegged at the rim when the basket has been completed.)

The techniques for carving the rim are the same as those for shaping the handle. A rim piece is ordinarily as wide as the top two weavers and thick enough (¼″ to ½″) to be beveled and shaped on the outside into a piece of half-round molding. It is important to make a neat scarf joint at the closing of the two overlapping ends (Fig. 4-8). Leave a 2½″ to 3″ allowance on each end for the overlap.

The rim liner for the inside of the basket is usually a double-thickness splint. When the rim and the liner are attached to the basket, their respective joins are placed at opposite sides of the basket.

Very early baskets were not, of course, nailed. Occasionally, one finds an old basket that has had the junction of the rim and the handle pegged. If nails are to be used, it is a good idea to drill pilot holes for the nails, or brads, first: bastard-cut wood splits easily. An old method of nailing rims consisted of heating the nails to a dull red in a fireplace and then plucking them out of the coals with pliers and driving them into the wood. Small nails, preferably non-rusting, can be driven through the wood, the point bent into a curve with pliers, and then clinched by hammering the curve against a piece of heavy metal. Most mountain basket-makers, it should be noted, frown on the use of nails.

4-7

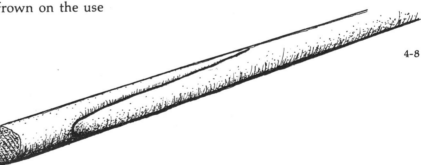

4-8

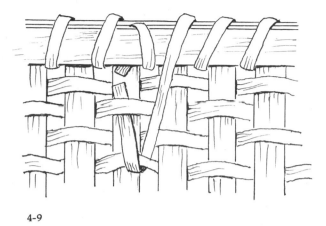

4-9

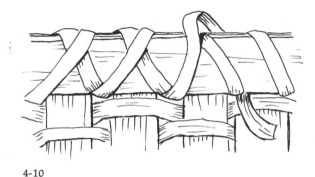

4-10

Rims are lashed in place with a ¼" to ⅜" ribbon of very thin splint (Figs. 4-9, 4-10). I use metal spring clamps to hold the rim pieces together while doing the lashing. Start the beginning of the lashing just beyond the scarf joint on the rim to allow for adjustment.

The small dowel often seen at the top of the rim assembly serves to make a very secure border lashing. The dowel is cut as a square ¼" or ⅛" strip from a double-thickness splint. some are left in their square shapes, while others have had their corners rounded. Overlap them two inches and scarf the joint.

LIDS

Lids are rare on splint baskets. A "trunk lid" type of cover is occasionally found on large, straight-sided rectangular wool storage baskets and on round sewing baskets.

In both cases, they are made exactly like the base of the particular basket, with a slight extra margin to permit them to clear the sides of the basket with ease.

The exterior rim on the basket is omitted to facilitate the passage of the lid sides. Unless a heavy reinforcement splint is lashed to the inside of the basket border, the rectangular baskets will be utterly shapeless. The turned-down sides of the lid may, or may not, have a rim piece lashed to the border. The rim liner on the lid is usually omitted.

These large, lidded rectangular baskets of splint are the least successful of all splint baskets. It is not the nature of thin oak or hickory to retain a freestanding shape without some added counterforce. The material wants to spring back into its original position; consequently, the baskets gap open on their long sides and curl up on the bottoms.

Lids are better suited to round baskets.

BASKET PATTERNS

A ROUND SERVICE BASKET (Plate 24, left)

Dimensions
Top diameter: 10"
Height: 4¾"
Height from center base to handle: 9½"
Handle from rim to rim: 16¾"

Materials
Seven 26" × ½" × ⅛" splints
One 26" × ¾" × ⅛" splint
About 16 yds. ¼" × 1/16" weavers
About 2 yds. ⅛" × 1/16" weavers
Rim and rim liner: 36" × ¾" double thickness
splint
Handle: 31½" long. ⅞" wide double thickness
splints

24. Left: round service basket, hickory handle and rims.
Right: two-pie basket, c. 1900. Rockbridge County,
Virginia. (Page 53.)

Base (7" diameter). Place a mark in the centers of each of the eight spokes. Soak well. Fold the spokes in half as shown in Fig. 4-11 and trim a small amount of the stock from the edges of the splint, from the center point to a distance of about 3". Snip a small sliver from each side of the fold, across the fold, to make a small notch when the splint is unfolded. This small V-shaped notch can be cut with a knife with the splint flat, but do not cut it too deeply (Fig. 4-12).

Trim *one end* of the wide ¾" splint to ½". Label this stake #7. Split #1 stake to within 1" of the center and, working on a flat surface, line up the spokes as indicated in Fig. 4-13, with the notches facing upward.

Using a paper-thin weaver, trimmed to a width of ⅛" for about a yard, slip the end under the first section of the split in spoke #1, as shown in Fig. 4-14. Randing clockwise around the center, try to keep the beginning rounds equidistant, 1" from the center, and snugly woven.

After the second round of weaving, tighten the weaver until the center rises to a slight peak. The notches facilitate this. A well-made round basket bottom should sit on the outside edges of the base.

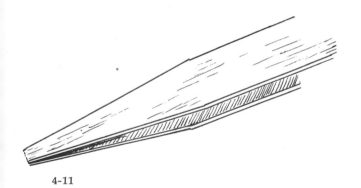

4-11

4-12

After the fourth or fifth round (or until a little space has opened up between the spokes) split the other end of spoke #1 with the scissors, split the *wide* end of spoke #7 into three ¼" pieces, and split each end of the remaining six spokes. (Fig. 4-15). There should now be thirty-three ¼" spokes in all. The widths of the weavers for the remainder of the base are widened after 1" of weaving to ¼". Overlap all new weavers, through two stakes, and conceal the ends (see Fig. 4-2). Weave until base measures 7" in diameter.

Sides. Score the stakes and upsett them for the sides. Allow the stakes to splay outward slightly. (The basket can be woven over a form of the proper size, such as a cooking vessel, or the tops of the stakes can be tied by pair-weaving a piece of string around them; however, this is usually more trouble than it's worth. You can give the sides of the basket a graceful shape with your hands alone and a little practice.)

As each round is woven, and after every other row is in place, pack the rows tightly against one another. Use the flat blade of a screwdriver as a tool. When the top is reached, allow the basket to dry *thoroughly*; the weavers will pack down as much as two or three rows from shrinkage. Add the additional rows to the basket. Soak the protruding stakes well and tuck alternate stakes to the inside (see Fig. 4-3). Trim the standing stakes level with the top weaver.

Handle. Prepare a curved handle. Taper the ends for 10" to a point that is about ¼" wide at the ends. Attach the handle as illustrated in Fig. 4-7.

Rim. Scarf the ends of the rim and the rim liner. Clamp in place over the top two rows of weaving and double-lash them with a fine ¼" splint (see Figs. 4-9, 4-10).

4-13

4-14

4-15

A PROVENDER BASKET (Plate 25)

Dimensions
Diameter: 18″

Materials
Seven 22″ × 1″ × ⅛″ splints
One 22″ × 1½″ × ⅛″ splint
About 15 yds. ⅜″ × 1/16″ weavers
Handle: 36″ × 1″ × ⅛″.

Base. Fold splints in half and trim to ¼″ width at centers (Figs. 4-11, 4-12). Make small notches at centers. (See the preceding directions for the round service basket). Trim one end of the wide 1½″ spoke to a width of 1″. Label this spoke #7. Split another spoke, called #1, to within ½″ of center. Line up spokes on a flat surface as in Fig. 4-13, notches facing upward.

Trim beginning weaver to ¼″ and insert end through split in spoke #1 (see Fig. 4-14).

Rand for 1½″, adding wider weavers as the distance between radiating spokes increases.

Split the wide end of spoke #7 into three ½″-wide strips and split the wide end of #1 and all other spokes, making a total of thirty-three ½″ spokes (see Fig. 4-15). Continue weaving until the diameter reaches 18″.

Trim and thin the ends of the stakes. Fold over alternate stakes and tuck in (see Fig. 4-3) on the bottom side of the basket. Cut remaining stakes. Place basket on a piece of twine, set a heavy weight, such as a rock, in the center, and draw the twine around the basket to curve the edges of the opposite sides. Allow the basket to dry into shape.

Handle: Prepare a smooth handle strip. Trim stock from ends and insert through several rows of weaving on outer surface of basket. Attach ends of handles as shown in Fig. 4-7.

Rim. This basket has neither rim nor liner. Double-lash the border over the last row of weaving.

25. Provender basket. This basket is known also as a sandwich basket or a flower basket. The style is from the mid-nineteenth century.

A ROUND SEWING BASKET (plate 26, right)

Dimensions
Top diameter: 10"
Height: 4½"

Materials
Sixteen splints 20" × ⅜" × 1/16"
Two handle pieces 8" × ⅜" × ⅛"
About 15 yds. ¼" very thin weavers
Lid: sixteen 14½" × ⅜" × 1/16" splints

26. Left: small basket of poplar; white-ash handle and
rims. Right: sewing basket, c. 1930.

Base. This basket has a sixteen-spoke base. Taper the centers of the base splints for about 6″. Split one spoke to within ½″ of center. Arrange eight spokes as in Fig. 4-16. Slip the end of a weaver, trimmed to a width of ⅛″, into the split stake and begin randing weave around the center of the base (Fig. 4-17). Weave about four rows until enough space has opened up to receive the other eight spokes. Lay each of the new spokes, successively, in the alternate spaces and weave them in (Fig. 4-18). There are now thirty-three spoke ends. Weave base to 8½″ diameter.

Sides. Soak and upsett side spokes. Loosen weavers slightly to create rounded sides. Tighten after weaving is 1½″ high. Weave until basket sides are 4¼″ high.

Rim. Tuck alternate stakes to inside (see Fig. 4-3). Cut off remaining stakes. Prepare ⅛″-thick rim liner to cover two rows of top weaving. Scarf ends and place *inside* top of basket.

(This basket does not have an outside rim piece.) Clamp the rim liner in place and single-lash through the second row of weaving with a ¼″ piece of very thin splint.

Lid. Make lid identical to base, but instead of peaking the *center* of the lid, pull the last 1½″ of weaving tighter to create a slight coning of the entire lid. Weave until the diameter of the lid measures 9½″.

Soak stake ends, place lid over basket, bend stakes down over sides, and weave sides of lid to a depth of 1½″. Shave alternate stake ends until they are quite thin and tuck to inside of lid. Cut standing stakes. (Lid has neither rim nor rim liner.) Double-lash the lid border over one row of weaving with a ¼″-wide piece of thin splint.

Handles. Shave 3″ on each end of the two handle pieces. Insert them on opposite sides of the lid, as shown in Figure 4-19.

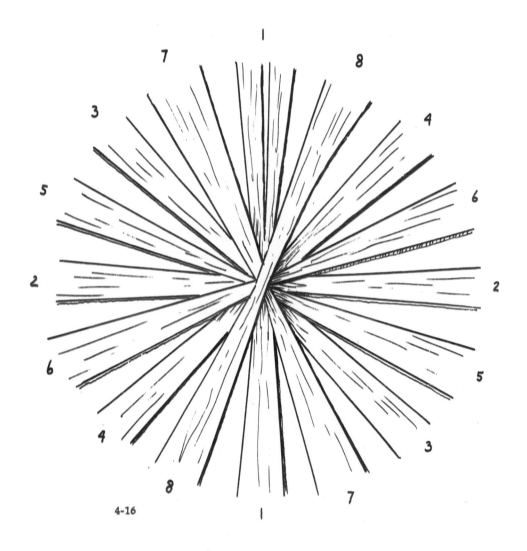

4-16

50

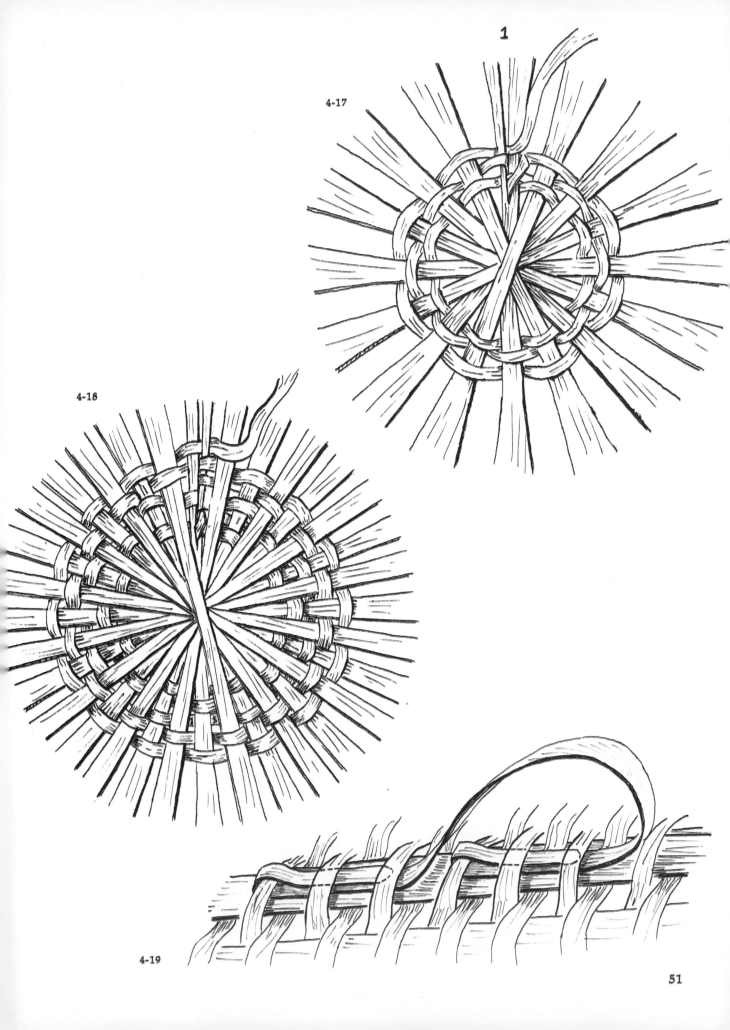

1

4-17

4-18

4-19

"GRAY SPLINTS" (Plate 27)

Dimensions
Diameter: 8"
Height: 6"
Handle from rim to rim: 12½"
Handle: 23" × ¾" × ½" (thick)
Rim and rim liner: 32" × ⅜" × ¼" (liner is ⅛" thick)

Materials
Sixteen 23" × ½" × ⅛" splints
13 yds. ⅜" × 1/32" weavers
3 yds. ¼" × 1/32" weavers
1 yd. ⅛" × 1/32" weaver

All of the weavers should be fully smoothed and trimmed to size. The rim lashing must be prepared, too. Dye all of these according to the instructions given on page 105 for dyeing gray with white oak bark. Dry the weavers for forty-eight hours after dyeing. Dampen slightly before using.

Base. The base is woven according to the instructions given for the round sewing basket, page 49. Begin with fine weavers and increase sizes as the base is woven. The diameter is 8".

Sides. Upsett the stakes. Continue randing weave with the gray splints. Do not add bulge to the sides. The sides may be splayed outward slightly, but retain a straight line rake. Weave the checkered pattern until the sides are 6" high. Dry the basket, pack down weavers, and tuck in alternate stakes (see Fig. 4-3).

Handle. Mark off 4½" on each end of the handle piece. Just above the marks carve a ½"-wide rim shelf, 3/16" deep (see photograph). Trim the remaining stock from the handle. Insert the handle ends into the weaving on the inside of the basket.

Rim. Scarf rim and liner and lash in place to the top row of weaving.

27. "Gray splints" basket, c. 1960. West Virginia.

A TWO-PIE BASKET (Plate 24, right)

Dimensions

18½″ × 9½″ × 3¼″
Handle from rim to rim across the top: 20¼″

Materials

Seventeen 17½″ × ⅝″ × ⅛″ splints
Nine 26½″ × ⅝″ × ⅛″ splints
Four 60″ × ⅝″ × 1/16″ weavers
Eight filler strips, about 21½″ long (width to be determined at the completion of the basket)
Rim and rim liner: 61″ × ⅝″ × ⅛″ (double-thickness splint)
Rim dowel: 61″ long, ¼″ thick
Handle: 36½″ × 1″ × ¼″

Base (18¼″ × 9¼″). Measure and mark centers of each splint and 4″ at each end of all splints. Soak splints well.

Pin or tape the first long splint to a flat board (see Fig. 4-1). Lay a short splint on *top* of this at right angles to the long one, leaving the 4″ margins protruding. Interweave all other splints, adding one at a time and taping the splints to the board to hold the stakes at right angles to one another, if necessary. Because of the equal thickness of the base splints, they will not close together. Be certain that the open spaces remain equidistant: filler strips will be added to the base to close the gaps after the basket has been completed and dried. Center the middle long and short splints so that the

handle will balance the basket. Resoak the protruding margins with a wet sponge.

Sides. Score the stakes evenly and upsett them. Drive finishing nails into the board at the outer edges of the four corners. Tie the tops of the splints around the nails with string, if desired.

Begin randing weave at the left-hand corner of a long side. Insert end of first weaver behind the second stake from the left (Fig. 4-20). (This basket is not woven spirally; each row is composed of a separate weaver.) Rand all around the first row, over an even number of stakes, and overlap the end of the weaver behind the beginning of the weaver, through the same spokes to the fifth stake, as shown in the illustration. (The first row will be difficult to tighten until the second or third rows are in place; make adjustments at that time.)

Start the second-row weaver at the opposite left-hand side of the basket. Alternate sides in this way until the four rows of weaving have been completed. Allow the basket to dry.

Handle and Rim. This basket has an unusual lashing technique. Each stake has had a ¼″ hole burned through the center of the wood at the edge of the top weaver. The char has been whittled out to receive the lashing (Fig. 4-21). This method makes for a very strong rim attachment.

4-20

4-21

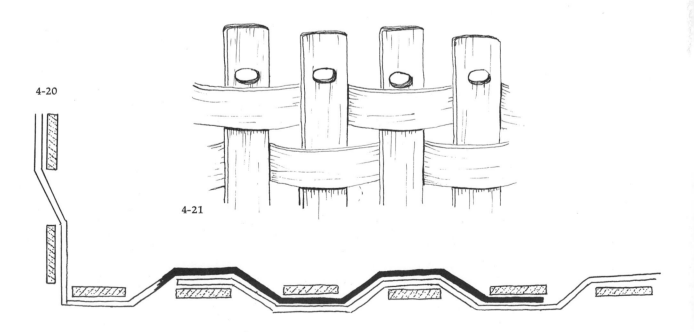

The holes should be made before the handle is attached. A woodburning tool or an *old* Phillip's head screwdriver (wooden-handled), heated to a dull red, will serve to char the holes. After the holes have been made, the tops of all the stakes are cut off ⅝" above the top of the last weaver.

Dress the handle piece and mark off 8" on each end. Shave the ends to a thickness of ⅛" and slype them. Bend the handle into an arc. Insert the end through the weaving on the outside of the center stakes of the long sides. Bend the handle ends carefully around the bottom edge of the basket. Insert the ends through the weaving to the center of the bottom. Cut a 6" piece of thin splint and work it through the weaving to lock the handle join in place across the bottom. (Use a screwdriver to force an opening for the insertions.)

Place the rim and the rim liner in position after bending them into the necessary rectangular shape. The ends should be overlapped and scarfed. The joins are centered at the handles—the rim on one side of the basket and the liner on the other side. Clamp the rim and liner in place with spring clamps or with several clothespins.

A very thin, ¼" ribbon of splint is now inserted into the weaving and the lashing proceeds as in Fig. 4-22. The rim dowel should be held by the hand until the lashing locks it in place. Mold the rim dowel around the corners as the lashing moves around the basket top. The rim dowel join is centered over a handle and the lashing begins just beyond this point to allow for adjustment in length of both the rim and the dowel as the wrapping by the splint proceeds.

Filler Strips. Slype the ends of the dampened filler strips and, beginning with the center lengthwise split, weave a slender filler through the same stakes on each side of the central stake. Filler strips are meant to close the gaps in the base. They should be slightly wider than the open spaces to be filled because, upon drying, they will shrink cross-grain. Work the pointed ends up underneath the side weavers of the basket, or cut them off flush with the bottom edge of the basket. Working outward from the center stake, skip every other stake and add fillers to each side of the alternate stakes. When the fillers have all been added, a pattern will emerge like that in Fig. 4-23. Should a gap remain between the last base splint and the side weaver, add a single filler to that space, also.

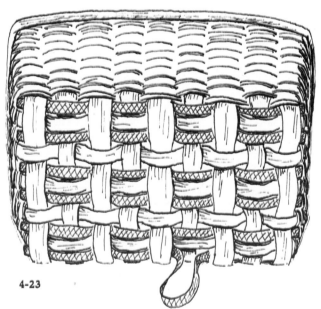

4-23

4-22

54

A RECTANGULAR MARKET BASKET
(Plate 17, top right)

Dimensions
13" × 9" × 7"
Handle from rim to rim across the top: 16½"

Materials
Nine 29" × ⅝" × ⅛" splints
Thirteen 27" × ⅝" × ⅛" splints
About 25 yds. ⅜" × 1/16" weavers
Ten filler strips, about 14½" long
Rim and rim liner: 46" long; 1" wide
Handle: 41" long

Base (9" × 11"). Align the base splints on a board and interweave them in a randing pattern, as in Fig. 4-1. Center the middle splints and be certain that the weaving elements are at true right angles. Drive finishing nails at the four corners as described on page 39.

Sides. Rewet the stakes with a damp sponge and upsett the stakes. Split one stake on the narrow end of the basket (see page 40). Insert a narrow weaver at the far left-hand side of one of the long sides and begin randing weave. Tighten weavers around nails and pack each round against the lower round tightly. Join weavers as shown in Fig. 4-2. The sides are 7" high. Allow the basket to dry before completing the top. Resoak the protruding stakes and complete the "tucking in" as shown in Fig. 4-3.

Handle. Prepare a notched handle piece. The notch may face either in or out of this basket (Fig. 4-24). Bend the handle into an arc and insert the ends into the centers of the long sides. Attach the rim and the liner and lash the rim pieces as shown in Fig. 4-9. Complete the handle attachment at the bottom of the basket (see Fig. 4-7), or insert handle ends through the weaving on the base to the middle of the bottom. Work filler strips lengthwise of the basket base to close all gaps in the weaving (see Fig. 4-23).

4-24

A TWILL WEAVE MARKET BASKET
(Plate 28)

Dimensions
Top: 18½" × 11¼" × 7"
Handle across top from rim to rim: 23"
Center height from base: 13⅛"

Materials
Twenty-four 29" × ⅝" × ⅛" splints
Ten 37" × 1" × ⅛" splints
Fourteen 62" × ½" × 1/16" weavers
Rim: 62" × ¾" × ⅜"
Rim liner: 61" × ¾" × ¼"
Handle: 37" × ¾" × ⅜"

Base (17" × 9¼"). Trim a slight amount of stock from the sides of each of the 1" splints. Mark centers and align the ten long splints side by side on a base board. Interweave the shorter splints in a twill pattern (see Fig. 1-4):

First row: over one, under two, over two, etc.
Second row: under two, over two, etc.
Third row: under one, over two, under two, etc.
Fourth row: over two, under two, etc.

Keep pattern established by checking diagonal lines. After the twenty-four splints have been woven into the base, squeeze the weaving elements together tightly and true the base to a right angle. Place a straightedge over the splints of the base perimeter and score the protruding ends for the upsett. Drive in the finishing nails at the four corners of the base.

28. Twill-weave market basket, c. 1910. Greenbrier County, West Virginia.

Sides. Upsett all stakes. Begin weaving the twill pattern at the twelfth stake on the long side—back of two, over two, etc. Overlap the ends of the weavers at the conclusion of the round through four or five stakes, concealing the two ends. Begin second round of weaving on the opposite side of the basket, stepping back one stake to maintain the diagonal pattern. Allow the side stakes to splay outward very slightly as the sides are woven. (Check top dimensions.)

Tuck in alternate top stakes (see Fig. 4-3).

Handle. This basket has a rectangular, carved handle (Figs. 4-24, 4-25). Plane the handle piece to a thickness of ⅜". Smooth the inside chamfers. Mark the center and the two corners underneath at the top, 11" apart. Working on the underneath side, carve out ⅛" of the stock of the inside of the corners to an even taper. Cut a ¾" wide dado notch on each inside beginning 6" down from the inside corner. The notch should be just deep enough to clasp the rim liner. A notch that is too deep will weaken the handle (which is why the handle broke on the basket in the photograph).

After the notches have been cut, taper the ends of the handle from the lower edge of the notch to a thickness of ⅛" at the tips.

Dip the mid-section of the handle piece into boiling water for about fifteen minutes; then slowly bend the corners. Tie the ends with string and set aside to dry into a square shape.

Rim. Fit the outside rim and the rim liner to the top of the basket, scarfing joins and bending the rectangular corners rather sharply.

Insert handle ends into the inside weavers at spoke 12 on one side of the basket and at spoke 13 on the other. Place the rim liner into the handle notches and the rim in position on the outside. Clamp. Single-lash snugly with a thin piece of ⅜"-wide splint.

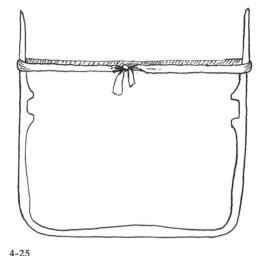

4-25

A BROWN MELON-SHAPED EGG BASKET
(Plate 29)

Dimensions
Diameter: 10"

Materials
Two rims 36½" × 1" × ¼"
Ten ribs 16" × 1" × ⅛"
About 14 yds. ¼" wide very thin splints (1/32")
for weavers
(See Chapter 8 on dyestuffs for dyeing splints)

Soak rim pieces for twenty minutes until they are very pliable. Bend rims into smooth circles by forming over the knee, working along the entire length. Overlap and fasten ends with clamps. Set aside to dry into circular shapes.

Mark off 2½" on each end of the overlap. This will leave 31½" for the rim circumference. Scarf ends (see Fig. 4-8) to form a continuous thickness. (The vertical rim should be adjusted to be about ½" smaller than the horizontal rim.)

After the circular frames have set to shape, recheck the measurements of the circles, then mark and cut two small notches, about 1" apart, in the edges of the overlaps. Tie the notches with a thin, well-soaked piece of splint about ⅛" wide. (A small clinched nail or a piece of wire can be used to tie the rims, also.)

Measure and mark off the half-way points on the insides of both hoops. Place the vertical rim *inside* the horizontal rim. The joins are placed on the center bottom and at one of the crossed intersections of the rims, respectively.

29. Melon-shaped egg basket in hickory, dyed dark brown. The style of the basket is English. An excellent example of "fourfold-bond" lashing.

Holding the rim bools at right angles with one hand, begin the fourfold bond lashing (Figs. 4-26, 4-27) with a well-soaked weaver. Make four or five complete revolutions around the four arms; clamp the weaver against the rim and repeat this operation on the other side of the basket.

Taking up four pairs of the ribs, taper the ends to a point and insert them into the pockets formed by the lashing. These ribs must be equal to the length of the bottom central rib, from rim to rim. It is important to keep this basket in the shape of a perfect sphere. This has to be done mostly by eye, but by careful fitting and trimming of the ribs, it can be done. Guard against letting the basket assume an elliptical shape.

Release the spring clamp, tighten the weaver, and begin over and under (randing) weaving, taking an extra turn over the rim at each side. Push each row firmly against the last, without rippling the weavers. Join new weavers in the central section of the weaving, not at the rims.

After six rows, or until enough space has opened up, add the other pair of ribs in the spaces just below the rim. Shorten these by careful measurement to maintain the spherical shape. Conceal the sharpened points of the rib ends under the weavers (see photograph). Continue randing to lock the new ribs in place. Work both sides, alternately, toward a mid-point on the basket's rim.

When all of the space has been filled with weaving, set the basket aside for twenty-four hours to dry. Work extra "packing" weaving into the center section, if necessary. Finish off the weavers by tucking them to the inside—under two weavers and back over one—or weave them through the randing on the inside of the basket, and cut off.

Rewet the basket; wedge a 10" piece of scrap wood across the diameter at the rim and another 10" piece between the handle and the bottom of the basket. This will allow the basket to dry into shape.

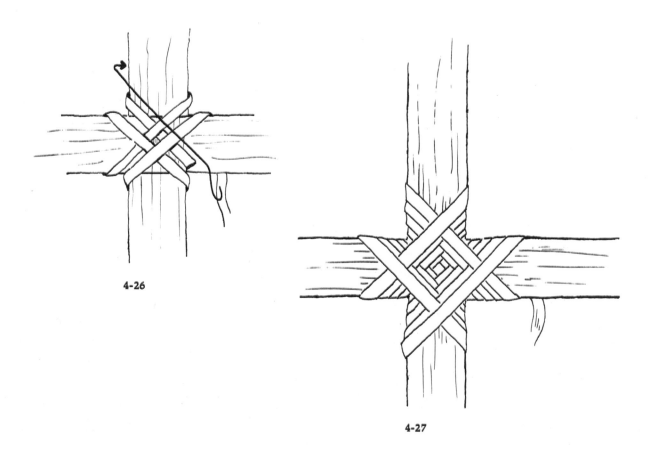

4-26

4-27

POTATO BASKET (Plate 30, center)

Dimensions
Diameter: 18"

Materials
Three ribs 30" × 1" × ⅛" (A, B, and C)
Two ribs 28" × 1" × ⅛" (D)
Two ribs 25" × 1" × ⅛" (E)
Two ribs 23" × 1" × ⅛" (F)
Two ribs 19" × 1" × ⅛" (G)
About 20 yds. ½" × 1/16" weavers
One rim piece, 10' long, double-thickness splint

Bend the rim piece over the knee, forming it into a circular shape. Scarf the two ends and overlap the rim to form a double-thickness circle whose circumference measures 56½". Clamp.

30. Left: service basket, twentieth-century copy of a style of basket that has been in this country since Colonial days. The basket type has been traced to the fourteenth century in the British Isles. They were commonly made in nests of three or four baskets. Center: white-oak potato basket. Right: hen basket from West Virginia. (Page 62.)

Taking up the three longest ribs (Fig. 4-28, A, B, and C), form them into a semicircular shape. Insert the ribs, parallel to one another and about 1" apart, between the two rim strips. (The ends of the rim will overlap one group of ribs.) Clamp the ribs in place and recheck the measurements. The basket is hemispherical and the three added ribs will measure about 28" from rim to rim.

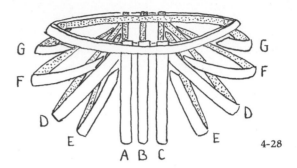

4-28

Insert a thin weaver, trimmed to ⅜", down beside the far left-hand rib (Fig. 4-29) and begin to cross-lash the three ribs in place (Figs. 4-30, 4-31). Pull the weaver tightly and take an extra turn or two around the rim pieces between the ribs to ensure that they are lashed securely.

After the third rib has been lashed in place, bring the weaver over top of the rim, give it a half-twist, and begin to rand across the ribs and up over the rim on the left side. Weave back and forth for two rows. Clamp the weaver to the rim and repeat the lashing at the opposite side of the basket.

Each side of the basket will have the empty spaces between the first group of three and

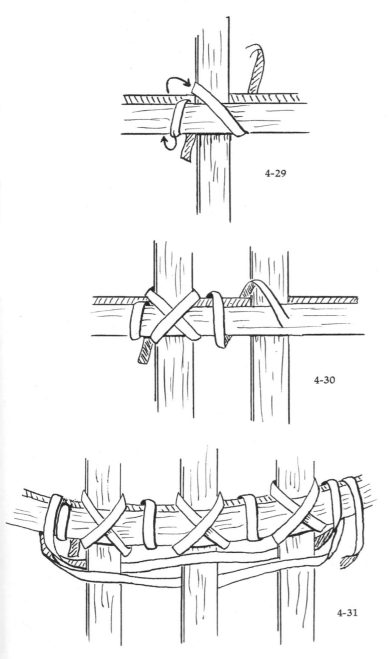

4-29

4-30

4-31

the rim evenly divided by the gradual insertion of four pairs of ribs, each pair being added at the same time.

Take up the D ribs, cut their ends at an angle so that they will abut the outside edges of ribs A and C, and sandwich them between the rim pieces next to A and C. Continue weaving for another three or four rows to lock the new ribs in place. Take an extra turn over the rim on each side. (The curve of the rim requires this extra fullness. Near the conclusion of the basket, some "packing," as shown in Fig. 5-5, may be necessary. Usually this is woven in before the final three or four rows. It is desirable on ribbed baskets to have the last rows woven straight across from one rim to the other.) Clamp the weaver to the rim and repeat at the opposite side of the basket. Alternate sides, in this way, as the basket is woven, always working toward the midpoint on the basket rims.

Add E rims by inserting their sharpened ends into the weaving halfway between C and D on one side and A and D on the other. Conceal ends beneath weavers. Weave two more rows.

Add F ribs between D and G. Weave two rows, and add G ribs between F and the rim.

At this point readjust D, E, F, and G to make them equidistant. Make certain that they form the spheroid curve of the basket. If a rib appears to be too long, insert an awl into the weaving along the side of the rib. Leave the awl in place to keep the weave open while the rib is eased out. Trim the end of the rib and reinsert it.

All adjustments in lengths of the ribs must be made at this time while they are fairly loose. Once the weaving progresses, they will become tightly locked into position.

Continue to rand on alternate ends of the basket. When only 4" remain open at the rim, wrap tightly across the space with the weaver and continue with that weaver down on the other side of the opening. At the same time, wrap across the other rim and continue weaving. It will be seen that the weavers will have exchanged sides after the rims have been wrapped. The weaving now continues, with the weavers turning over G ribs. This creates the handle opening.

If an uneven gap remains in the bottom of the basket, fill it in with "packing." Take the weaver over successively lower ribs in a stepwise fashion until the open space is even from rim to rim. Continue weaving straight across between the rims until all space has been tightly filled. Lock the concluding ends of the weavers underneath other weavers, or weave them away through the weaving at right angles.

A HEN BASKET (Plate 30, right)

Dimensions
15½" high

Materials
One rim 60" × ½" × ⅛"
Two rims 33" long, rounded ¼" dowels
Two ribs 44" × ¼" × ⅛"
Two ribs 40"
Two ribs 38"
Two ribs 36"
Two ribs 32"
Two ribs 27"
Two ribs 20"
Two ribs 15"
Two ribs 12"
Two ribs 9"
¼" thin weavers

The basket is woven from the top downward.

Form the center (½"-wide) rib into a circle, 48" in circumference. Overlap scarfed ends and tie on notches with thin splint, or clinch-nail it at the center top. Form the two rims of the opening into circles, 29" in circumference. Scarf joints and tie.

Holding all three circles side by side at the top, loop a ½" weaver over the three rims at center top; clamp it in the center of the handle, and wrap the rims tightly toward one end of the handle (about 2½"), holding the three pieces flat (Fig. 4-32).

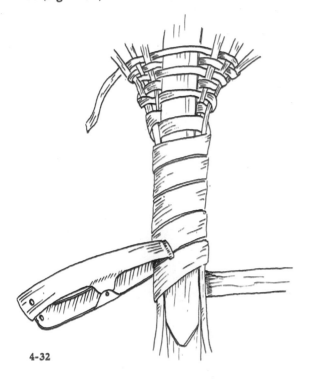

4-32

Begin randing weave through the three pieces for one row. Insert ends of the longest ribs next to the outer rims. (Always begin the weaving-in of the added ribs at the *conclusion* of a row in order to keep a regular randing pattern in the center section of the weaving. Skip over the newly added rib at the beginning of the row.)

As the weaving proceeds, ribs are added after each two rows of weaving. They are inserted next to the small rims; the ends are concealed beneath a weaver. The ribs are woven into the randing as soon as space opens up.

(Some hen baskets have the ribs inserted next to the main rib. This produces a basket that is wider at the bottom than the basket described here. Note the Scottish willow hen basket in Plate 5 (page 15).

When the weaver on the first side runs out, begin to work on the other side of the basket. Finish the handle wrapping and begin randing. Carefully measure the lengths of the ribs as they are brought around and inserted into the weaving; the pairs should match and the first four pairs of ribs should allow the basket to sit flat on the bottom. Some trimming of the ends of the ribs will be necessary.

After the first several ribs have been woven into the fabric, assess the overall shape of the basket. Decide upon the final outline of the form at this time. Rewet the basket, if necessary, to bend it into shape.

The bottom should be slightly flattened to keep it from rolling when it is set down. The curves of the sides may be quite variable. It is the tightness of the weaving and the number of ribs that will determine the final outline of the basket. Some basketmakers "brace" the ribs at the bottom of the basket by weaving three or four rows across it with scrap splints. (A row or two of pairing weave with honeysuckle will brace the framework, also.)

Continue weaving until the sides force the weavers to curve too much to keep the weaving close together near the rims of the openings. "Gussets" will be added at this point. They are formed by packing (see Fig. 5-5). In a stepwise progression, take the weaver over successively lower ribs, instead of the rims. Work back up again toward the rim and then downward once again. A V-shaped wedge will have been woven.

Weave straight across the bottom, from one rim to the other, until the basket is completed. Work each side toward a central point on the rims. Finish off weavers by threading them through the weaving on the inside of the basket.

A FLAT-BOTTOMED EGG BASKET
(Plate 31, left)

Dimensions
Circumference of vertical rim: about 31½"
Circumference of horizontal rim: 28"

Materials
Vertical rim: 34½" × 1¼" × ¼"
Horizontal rim: 31" × ⅝" × ¼"
Sixteen ribs 17½" × ¼" × ⅛"
Two ribs 15½" × ¼" × ⅛"
Two ribs 14" × ¼" × ⅛"
Two ribs 12" × ¼" × ⅛"
Two ribs 10" × ¼" × ⅛"
Two ribs 8½" × ¼" × ⅛"
¼" thin weavers

31. Left: flat-bottomed egg basket, c. 1910. Rockbridge
County, Virginia. Note the insertion of the ribs at the
rim. Right: honeysuckle copy of a nineteenth-century
English willow basket. (Base spokes are willow.)
Rockbridge County, Virginia. (Page 93.)

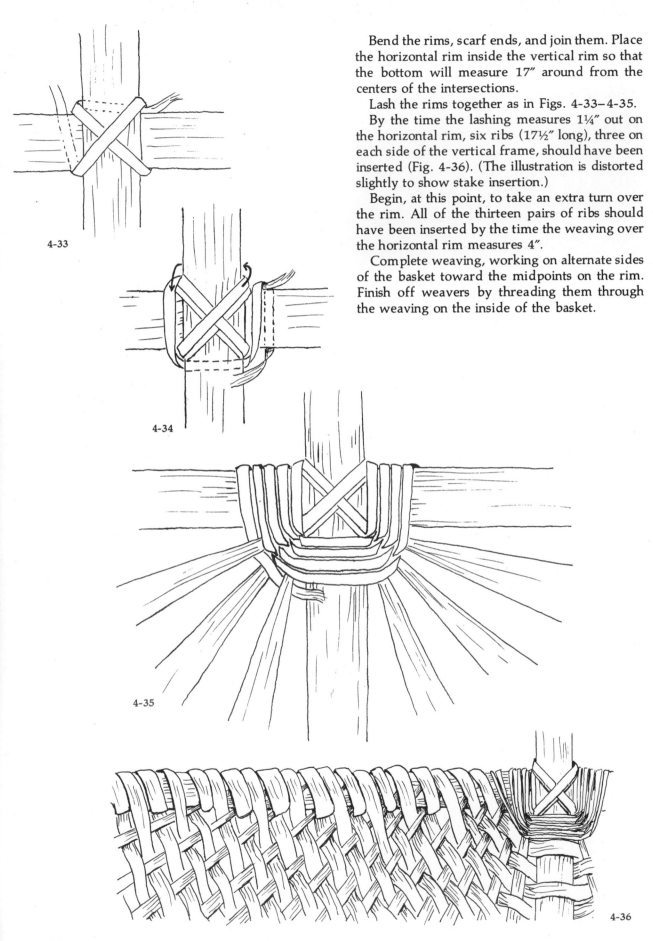

Bend the rims, scarf ends, and join them. Place the horizontal rim inside the vertical rim so that the bottom will measure 17" around from the centers of the intersections.

Lash the rims together as in Figs. 4-33–4-35.

By the time the lashing measures 1¼" out on the horizontal rim, six ribs (17½" long), three on each side of the vertical frame, should have been inserted (Fig. 4-36). (The illustration is distorted slightly to show stake insertion.)

Begin, at this point, to take an extra turn over the rim. All of the thirteen pairs of ribs should have been inserted by the time the weaving over the horizontal rim measures 4".

Complete weaving, working on alternate sides of the basket toward the midpoints on the rim. Finish off weavers by threading them through the weaving on the inside of the basket.

4-33

4-34

4-35

4-36

A TWIN-BOTTOMED EGG BASKET

Craft guilds of the past required a young man who had finished his apprenticeship to submit a piece of work for approval to the guild's examiners before the rank of "Master" was conferred upon him. The twin-bottomed egg basket is the "master piece" of splint basketry (see the frontispiece and Plate 32). There are no specific directions for making it. The reason for this is that no two basketmakers weave with the same degree of tension and, in this basket, the tightness of the weave over the compound curves determines the length and the number of ribs needed. The egg basket is literally designed while it is being made. (Do not attempt to make it before learning the techniques of rib work contained in the other rib baskets given in this chapter.) There are, however, some general guidelines for making it.

Make the rims at least ¼" thick.

The vertical rim is usually a few inches shorter than the horizontal rim.

The horizontal rim is seated above the bottom at about two-thirds of the distance of the total height.

The lashing in Figs. 4-33–4-35 is better suited to this many-ribbed splint basket than the four-fold-bond lashing in Figs. 4-26 and 4-27. The lashing strips are narrowed for the first three or four rows of weaving.

The first several pairs of ribs to be added should outline the curves of the twin bottoms. The ends of the ribs are pointed and thinned.

In order to accommodate all of the rib ends in the small space at the junction of the two rims, cross the ends of the first two pairs of ribs (the longest ribs) on the inside of the basket, concealing ends under lashing.

All of the ribs for the framework should be worked into place by the tenth row of weaving, if not sooner.

If the weaving from the fourth row to the tenth row is too tight, it will squeeze the ribs of the base curves into unsightly pouches. A pair of smoothly rounded curves is the idea. For a novice, it might be a good idea to brace the framework with some temporary weaving across the bottom to keep the skeleton of the basket rigid.

If no rim dowel is used, take the weaver an extra turn around the rim from time to time. This will prevent the dragging down of the horizontal rim.

Use narrow, fine weavers and add enough ribs to ensure a closely woven, tightly packed texture.

32. Twin-bottomed egg basket. The most common style of basket of the Appalachian Mountains.

Wickerwork

"Mrs. Hinkle used to tell that she give a gypsy woman a pan of fresh cornbread to teach her how to make a wicker basket like that."

A man from Virginia

Wicker, wicked, witch, and *willow* are derived from the same Anglo-Saxon stem, according to Robert Graves in *The White Goddess.* All of these words were intimately related in ancient folklore. Wickerwork baskets, made of the sacred willow, were used as ritual containers. Witches drove out evil spirits by beating the victim with willow or birch rods. The "Witch's Besom" broom is still made in England and in a few places in the Appalachians. The broom was originally composed of birch twigs, an ash or an oak handle, and bound with willow strips, and it is the same well-known conveyance used by elderly ladies of the moonlit Halloween sky.

Round-rod wickerwork baskets begin with an arrangement of crossed spokes at the center of the base called a "slath." Finer material is then woven over this framework. After the base has been woven, side stakes are either inserted into the weaving in the base and then bent upwards, or the base spokes themselves are bent upwards to form the framework for the sides.

There are many weaving patterns and a variety of border patterns used in wickerwork. The basic patterns used in Appalachian baskets are given below.

THE WEAVES

RANDING

Simple over and under weaving with a single weaver (Fig. 5-1). Randing requires an uneven number of stakes.

CHASING

Randing weave worked over an even number of stakes (Fig. 5-2). Two weavers are used alternately in the following way. The first weaver is laid in behind a stake and worked around to its beginning, stopping with the stake immediately to the left of the beginning stake. A second weaver is inserted at this point and worked around until it reaches the stake on the left of the first emerging weaver. The first weaver is now picked up and woven around. The two weavers continue to "chase" each other around the rows of randing weave.

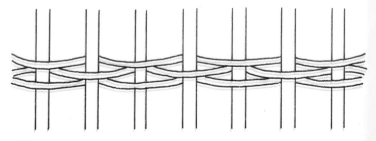

5-1

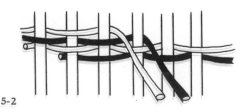

5-2

SLEWING

Slewing weave consists of two or more weavers worked together in a simple randing pattern (Fig. 5-3). Note that the first (lowest) pair of weavers is staggered to prevent the appearance of a hole.

FRENCH SLEWING

French slew is a diagonal randing pattern used with short willow rods, or any short rods (Fig. 5-4). The pattern avoids the weakening effect of constantly pieced short weavers and it provides greater uniformity in the sizes of the weavers.

Rods are laid in behind successive stakes and woven in randing weave up the sides of the basket in a diagonal direction. There will be as many weavers as stakes. The butt of the first rod is laid in behind the first stake and taken over one, under one. The next rod is placed behind the stake at the left and woven over one, under one, and so on around the basket. One randing stroke at a time is worked with consecutive weavers until the rods are worked out. Short rods will run out about midway up the basket sides. Level the weaving at this point, slype the ends, and leave them behind the stakes. Insert the butts of new weavers behind the stakes and continue weaving to the top of the basket.

French slew has a tendency to warp the basket. There are three ways to control this:

(1) Keep the spokes vertical and keep the tops of the weaving rounds as level as possible.

(2) Two or three rounds of waling (see page 68) can be worked midway, at the tops of the first concluding set of weavers. An arrow waling (see page 70) is a good stabilizer, also.

(3) The waling at the top border should be very sturdy and perfectly level.

PACKING

Packing (Fig. 5-5) is used to increase the sides or the base in specific areas. The technique may also be used to create "gussets" for curved areas, such as will be found in the hoods on cradles. Packing is used often with ribbed baskets of splint.

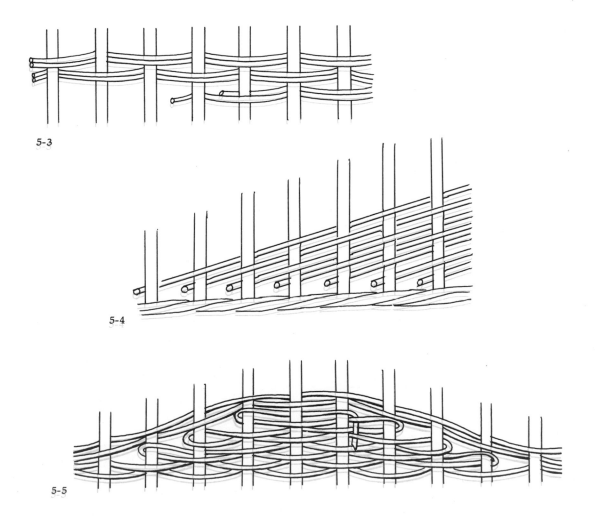

5-3

5-4

5-5

PAIRING

Pairing weave (Fig. 5-6) is started in either of the two ways shown: by doubling a weaver over the stake, or by inserting two weavers, behind two consecutive stakes. The weaver at the left, or the "back weaver," is passed over the "forward weaver," taken behind the next stake and out. Pairing weave can be given an extra clockwise twist between stakes when the stakes are far apart. (This is a useful weave for holding the tops of stakes in position for weaving the upsett of a basket.)

If a second round of pairing is given a counterclockwise twist (back weaver passing *under* the forward weaver), a pattern resembling a line of arrow results. (See arrow waling, page 70.)

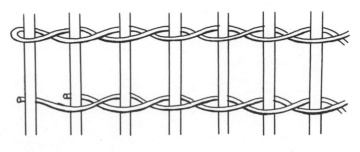

5-6

WALING

Wale weaving (Figs. 5-7–5-9) is extremely strong. For this reason, it is the pattern of choice for holding spokes securely at the upsett, for completing the weaving at the tops of baskets, and for providing reinforcement of the framework wherever it may be needed.

Basic three-rod wale is similar to pairing weave except that it is woven with three rods, instead of two. Three rods are inserted behind three consecutive stakes. The "back weaver" is taken in front of two stakes (to the right), behind the third stake and brought out to the front. The movement continues with the other weavers, always moving the far left-hand weaver forward over the tops of the weavers to the immediate right. A round of waling is completed when the beginning and the end of the weavers are resting, respectively, behind the same three stakes, although it is usual to bring the end of the weaver through to the outside, underneath the other two weavers before cutting it off. This gives the round of wale the appearance of a continuous piece of rope.

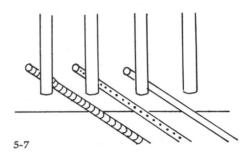

5-7

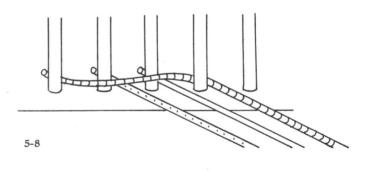

5-8

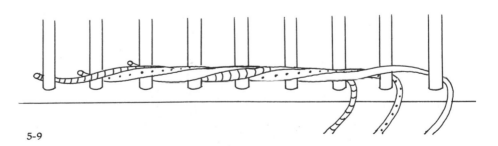

5-9

When working more than one round of waling, the marked spiral look of the wale as it steps up to the next round can be softened by a slight change of weaving at the end of each round. The progression of the weaving is reversed at this one point.

Carefully note the beginning stake, #1 (Fig. 5-10). When the round returns to #1, instead of taking weaver A in front of two stakes and back of #1, begin, at this point, with weaver C. Take C in front of two stakes and back of #3. Then take B over two and back of #2; then A is moved *twice:* in front of two and back of #1, and again, in front of two and back of #4. Normal waling proceeds.

Waling may be worked with more than three rods.

Four-rod wale is worked with four rods taken over *three* stakes and back of one. Similarly, five-rod wale is worked with five rods, each taken over *four* and back of one, and so on.

As a general rule, the larger the basket and the heavier the weaving elements, the larger the waling. For example, small baskets of vines or honeysuckle will be adequately supported by a three- or four-rod wale, while a large, heavy basket of willow will require a thicker four-, five-, or six-rod wale.

The change of weaving at the ends of rounds can be worked with any number of weavers in the wale. All that is necessary is a reversal of the progression of weavers at #1 spoke.

If the directions call for a change from four-rod wale to three-rod wale, the change-of-weaving is not worked. Instead, when the concluding end of the first weaver is resting behind #1 stake, it is brought forward (as usual) and cut off. The remaining three weavers complete their normal four-rod wale progression. (This completes the four-rod round). The three weavers will now be considered as members of a *new* round of three-rod wale and #2 stake of the old four-rod wale will be called "#1 stake" in the succeeding rounds of three-rod wale.

It is important to give close attention to the details of these changes in weaving patterns, confusing though they may be at first. The smoothness of the surface weaving depends upon concealing the points of change in the weaving as much as possible.

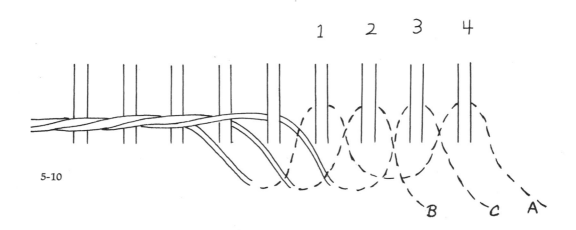

5-10

ARROW WALING

If, after one round of waling has been worked, the weavers of the second round are taken *underneath* one another, in a counterclockwise spiral, an arrow pattern results (Fig. 5-11). This is not only a strong weave, but also, depending upon its placement, a decorative line on the basket sides.

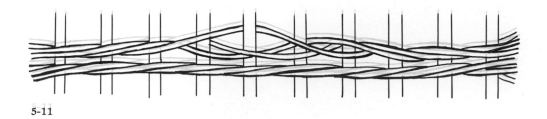

5-11

METHODS OF JOINING NEW WEAVERS

Fine weavers are best joined by having their ends tucked down into the weaving about ½" as shown in Fig. 5-12. Heavier rods will have their ends slyped and both will lie behind the same stake on the inside of the basket (Fig. 5-13), or the concluding weaver will be brought forward to the outside (Fig. 5-14). (Mountain baskets designed to hold wool or yarn have the weavers projecting on the outside of the basket, doubtless to avoid snags. A nicely slyped cut will accomplish the same purpose. The cut should be angled along the plane of the sides of the basket.)

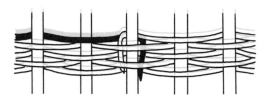

5-12

5-13

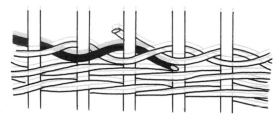

5-14

BASES

ROUND BASES

A round base is shown in Plate 31.

Begin by opening a slit through the centers of four rods. Insert four more rods through the cuts and insert one extra shortened rod into the slath at the corner (Fig. 5-15). (If the spokes are too small to slit, lay the rods on top of each other and add the extra spoke after a couple of rounds of pairing.)

Take up a weaver, bend it about one-third of its length, and fold it around four of the spokes. Proceed with pairing weave (Fig. 5-16). Pair, over four stakes at a time, around the slath twice (Fig. 5-17).

Separate the spokes into twos. Keep spokes damp in order to bend them into the spreading, radial formation. Treat the added spoke as a pair of spokes at this round. Continue pairing weave over the double spokes for one or two rounds. Spread the spokes farther apart and pair over single spokes for two complete rounds (Fig. 5-18).

Cut out one weaver and lodge its end beneath a spoke. Continue randing weave with the other weaver until the desired diameter of the base has been reached. (Directions occasionally call for a round or two of pairing or wale at the outer rounds of the base.)

Basket bottoms should be slightly convex to allow the basket to sit on the outer rim of the base. The saucer shape is attained by pulling the weavers tighter in the outer rows of weaving.

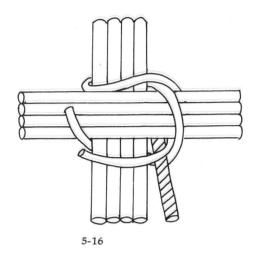

5-16

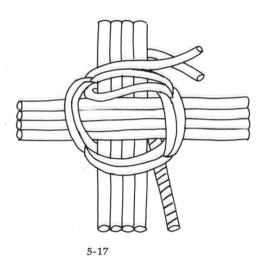

5-17

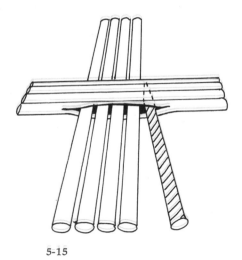

5-15

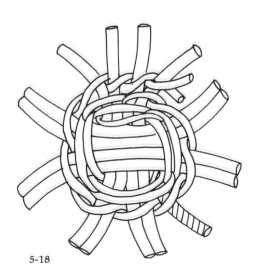

5-18

OVAL BASES

An oval slath is made by inserting a given number of long stakes through several evenly spaced short ones. In general, oval baskets need more stakes, closer together, at their ends to accommodate the curves. Stakes for the framework of the sides are usually inserted into the base, one on either side of the end stakes; however, stakes along the straight sides of the basket may be only single-staked. The distance between the stakes of the slath should account for this. For example, if the stakes of the slath are too close together on the long sides, the finished basket will take on an odd-looking rounded shape, rather than a true oval. If the stakes are too far apart, the fabric of the entire basket will be weakened.

Oval Base for Fine Materials (Fig. 5-19). Insert three (or more) long stakes through about nine short stakes. (Exact lengths will be given in the directions for the baskets.) The proper length of the slath is obtained by leaving equal lengths of the protruding stakes emerging from both the ends and the sides: the same amount of weaving must fill the space on the sides as well as the ends.

Two stakes are placed together at each end of the slath. The remaining stakes are evenly spaced between these.

Insert an extra stake at one end of the slath for an uneven number of stakes, or omit the extra stake and use two "chasing" weavers.

Insert the end of a fine weaver into the slot (A). Holding the stakes flat, wrap the weaver around the slath to the end. Add another weaver (B) and pair around the slath once or twice before spreading the end spokes. Pair over the end spokes individually as soon as space opens up. Continuous pairing weave on the bottom will warp an oval base. Cut out one weaver and change to randing weave as soon as the end spokes have been fanned out and locked into position. Weave base to desired size.

Oval Base for Willow (Fig. 5-20). Arrange stakes for slath as above. Instead of wrapping the slath, begin pairing weave at A and B as shown. Begin with the tips of the withes.

Willow will kink, and this characteristic helps it hold its position snugly. Change to randing as soon as possible (C).

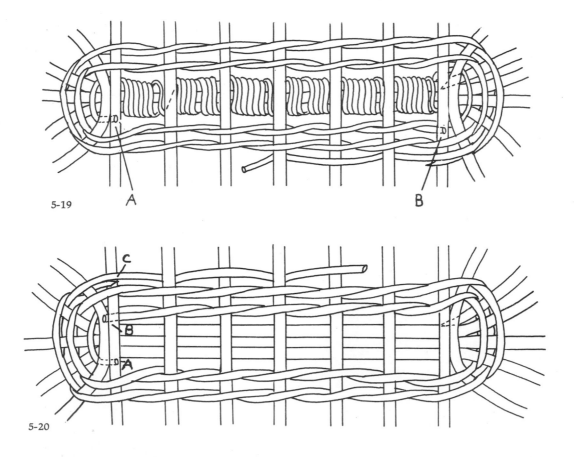

5-19   A   B

5-20

SQUARE OR RECTANGULAR BASES

Base for Fine Material (Fig. 5-21). Align stakes for the slath as shown in the illustration. The vertical stakes may be inserted *through* the horizontal stakes or simply placed underneath.

The lashing shown in the illustration is an easy one, but it may be varied to accommodate short lengths of weavers. Use any method that works!

After the slath has been made, begin randing weave around the protruding stakes, fanning out the corner stakes as the weaving proceeds.

Rectangular Base in Willow (randing weave).
Make a wooden clamping device (Fig. 5-22) for holding the withes upright from two pieces of 1" × 2" × 16" stock. Drill three holes through both pieces of wood. Use small carriage bolts, washers, and wing nuts to fasten the blocks

of wood together. (A C-clamp may be used to hold the block to a working table top.)

Lay the clamp on its side and insert stakes about 1" to 1½" apart. Use thicker spokes at each edge of the base. Slype their ends to equal the thickness of the other stakes. Tighten the clamp and set it upright.

Fold a weaver around the first spoke and pair across the base of the spokes. Cut out one of the weavers; wrap one and a half times around the end spoke, and rand back across.

Go to the tops of the spokes and repeat the pairing weave (or nail a small rod to the outer stakes with ¾" brads). This will hold the spokes rigid while the base is being woven.

Lodge slyped ends of weavers beneath spokes on the bottom side. Take an extra turn around the end spokes from time to time.

After the base is woven, remove it from the clamp and cut off the protruding ends flush with the weaving.

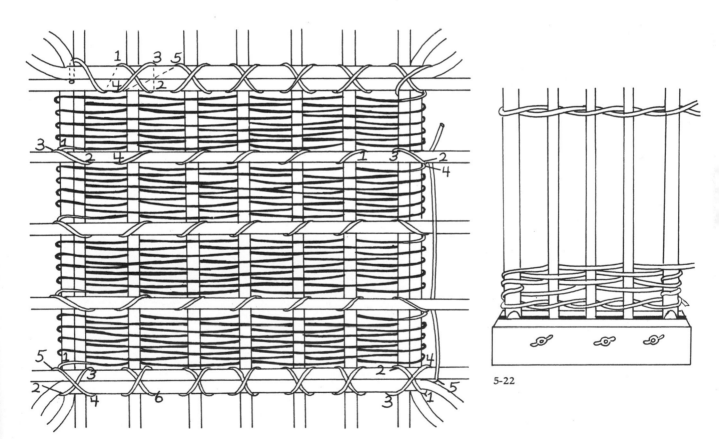

5-21

5-22

UPSETTING THE SIDES OF THE BASKET

UPSETTING ROUND BASKETS

Slype the ends of the stakes for the basket sides and insert them 1½" to 2" into the weaving on each side of the base spokes (Fig. 5-23). If the material is strong enough, or the basket small, a single stake will suffice. Facing the bottom of the basket, work a round of four- or five-rod wale. This will give the basket a firm edge to sit on and help to conceal the ends of the base spokes.

Set the basket upright. Score the stakes with the tip of a knife, and at the same time, give the stake and the knife a slight twist and bend the stake upward.

After all the stakes have been upsett, weave a loose band around the top of the basket to hold the stakes to the desired rake until the upsett wale has been woven. A circle of wire of the proper size, tied to several stakes, may be used. The final shape of the basket is determined at this point. After the wale is woven, the band can be removed.

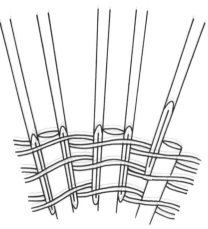

5-23

Continue wale weaving up the sides of the basket for two or three more rounds, remembering to change the progression of weaving at the beginning stake each time the wale steps up to another round (see Fig. 5-10).

It is customary to reduce the number of weavers in the wale at the beginning of the wale on the sides. For example, if a five-rod wale was used on the bottom, cut out the leading weaver, as described on page 69, and continue the wale on the sides with a four-rod wale.

The size of the rods for the wale should stand somewhere between the small weavers and the thicker stakes. If a particularly thick-looking wale is desired at the foot of the basket, cut and scarf a rod to fit around the perimeter of the base and use this rod as a core for the wale, wrapping the weavers over the core each time they emerge from behind a stake.

On large willow baskets with paired stakes, the bottom wale is woven over each *pair* of stakes. When the side wale is begun, the weavers are taken *between* the pairs, thus doubling the number of stakes. After the side wale has been finished and before the randing weave begins, by-stakes are slyped and inserted down into the wale alongside each stake. The extra stakes add considerable strength to the basket.

UPSETTING OVAL BASKETS

The curves at the ends of oval baskets, as mentioned before, require more fullness. End stakes and the first pair of stakes along the sides are usually double-staked. The remaining side spokes will be single-staked, unless the spokes of the base are too far apart. Obtaining a good shape on an oval basket requires a little practice. Examining nicely formed old baskets for the manner of staking is a good way to study the structure of oval baskets.

The staking, wale, and upsett are identical to that described for round baskets.

UPSETTING RECTANGULAR BASKETS

The randed rectangular base is treated as follows. Select side stakes and slype their ends. Make equidistant holes through the heavy outside spokes on the long sides of the base. The awl is pushed through the stakes at a slight upward angle. Soap the ends of the sharpened side stakes and insert them through the holes (Fig. 5-24); upsett the stakes by giving the withes a slight twist as they are bent upward.

Stakes on the other two ends are inserted into the weaving beside the base stakes.

Before beginning the upsett wale, cut four thicker corner posts. The posts should be measured from the bottom of the basket to the top of the weaving. The posts are set in place, at each outside corner, as the wale is woven. It may be necessary to trim the posts slightly at the lower edge to make them fit neatly.

Begin three-rod wale with the tips of the weavers as shown in Fig. 5-25. Anchor end of the first rod around the left-hand stake, as illustrated. The other two rods are laid in behind their respective rods, as usual. When the right-hand corner is reached, set the first post in position and weave it in as if it were another stake (Fig. 5-26). Two or three rounds of wale are worked before beginning randing weave. Before the tops of the stakes are bent down for the border, the corner posts are cut off flush with the top row of weaving and four border stakes, the size of the other stakes, are inserted by the corner posts for the border.

Wicker furniture makes extensive use of the techniques for this type of basket.

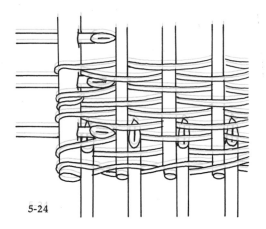

5-24

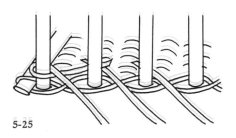

5-25

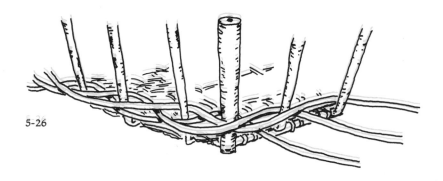

5-26

WEAVING THE SIDES

Weaves for the basket sides may be varied, but not to the point of creating a "busy" surface. A general rule of thumb is to have no more than three changes of pattern on the sides. Separate different patterns with a round or two of wale or arrow wale.

Bands of color and meander patterns should be worked out ahead of time so that the areas will be well-proportioned. Both color and patterned areas will stand out against the total area of the background of the basket. Give attention to the "negative space" in the area to be decorated.

Basketry is a species of architecture. There is no reason, certainly, why this architecture cannot be decorated, but the decoration should enhance the three-dimensional form, should *highlight* the total shape. If, for example, the basket is to have a curve three-quarters of the way up the side, a colored band should be introduced there, not at the half-way point. On the other hand, color and pattern can be used to *disguise* a mistake. To use the example of a curve again, let us assume that the prospect of a graceful curve at the top of a vase-shaped basket has been wrecked by starting the curve too late. If a few rows are taken out and a band of bright color is introduced, it will have the effect of drawing the eye lower on the side of the basket and this illusion will help to compensate for what is really a poorly shaped basket.

BORDERS

After the sides have been woven, it is usual to work two or three rounds of wale at the top before beginning the border. The stakes should be well dampened before they are bent.

CLOSED BORDER I

Step 1 (Fig. 5-27).   Starting anywhere around the top, take a stake (or a group of stakes) behind the next two stakes to the right and bring the end forward. Work this pattern around the basket. Thread the last standing stakes through the curves of the established pattern.

Step 2 (Fig. 5-28).   Take each protruding end, in turn, over three stakes and down through the curves formed by Step 1 (to the inside of the basket). Slype ends of stakes and make certain they are lodged behind the stakes to keep them from flipping forward out of the pattern.

Borders can be worked, after a little practice, with a definite rhythm. It is helpful to learn borders by repeating the pattern verbally. For example:

Step 1. "Behind-two-and-out."
Step 2. "Over-three-and-in."

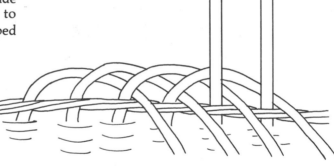

5-27

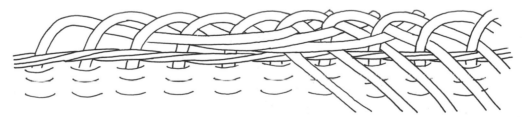

5-28

CLOSED BORDER II (for short ends)

One step: "Back-of-one, over-two-and-in" (behind next stake). (Figs. 5-29, 5-30).

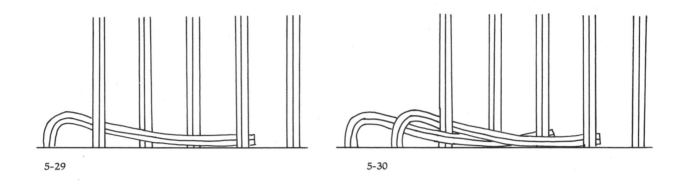

5-29

5-30

THREE-ROD PLAIN

Step 1. To begin the border, take three consecutive stakes "back-of-one-and-out." (Fig. 5-31).

Step 2. Take #1 stake over the next two, back of #5 stake, and bring it forward (Fig. 5-32). Take #4 stake back of #5 and bring it forward to the right of the end of #1 stake. Continue same pattern with each long, protruding end (Fig. 5-33).

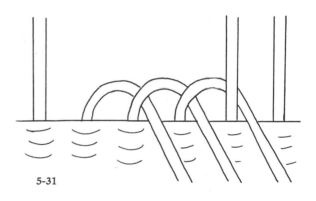

5-31

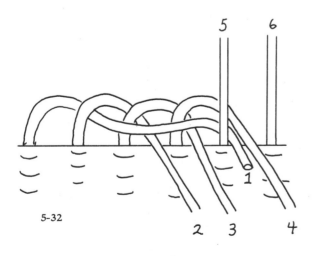

5-32

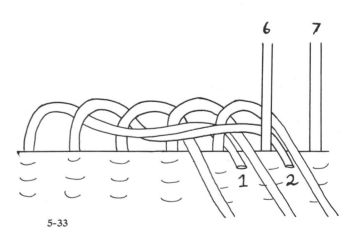

5-33

FOUR-ROD-BEHIND-TWO PLAIN

The four-rod-behind-two plain border is similar to the three-rod plain, except that the pattern is extended over more stakes.

Step 1. Take the first four standing stakes "behind-two-and-out." (Fig. 5-34).

Step 2. Take the end of #1 stake "over-three, back-of-one-and-out." (Fig. 5-35). Take #5 stake "behind-two-and-out" beside the end of #1 stake.

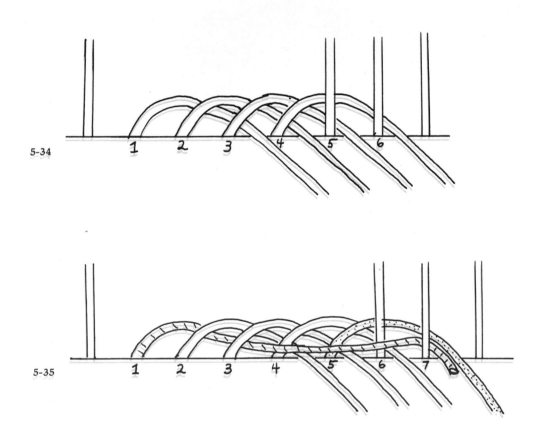

5-34

5-35

TWISTED ROPE BORDER (Plates 1 and 21)

The twisted rope border is not only simple to make; it is also ideal for heavy, unpeeled hardwood rods. It may be woven with only the upstanding rods, or extra rods can be inserted alongside the beginning stakes to make a thicker border The most common border in use with willow is given here.

Insert an extra rod into the weaving beside each of the first two border stakes. Giving the first pair a counterclockwise twist, take the rods in front of the next pair, to the right, and lodge ends (temporarily) behind the next single stake. Repeat with the second pair.

Return to the ends of the first pair; bring them forward on the right-hand side of the standing stake. Bend down the single stake and twist all three rods together. Take the three ends in front of the standing stake at the right and lodge them behind the next.

This establishes the movement of the twisted stakes around the border. Hereafter, each short end protruding on the inside of the basket is left (to be cut off later), and the new standing stake is added to the three-rod twist.

At the end of the border, thread the last pair under the beginning pair; then sew one rod from each of the last three-rod groups in and out of the grooves of the two sets of stakes at the beginning of the border. The border should resemble a continuous piece of loosely twisted rope.

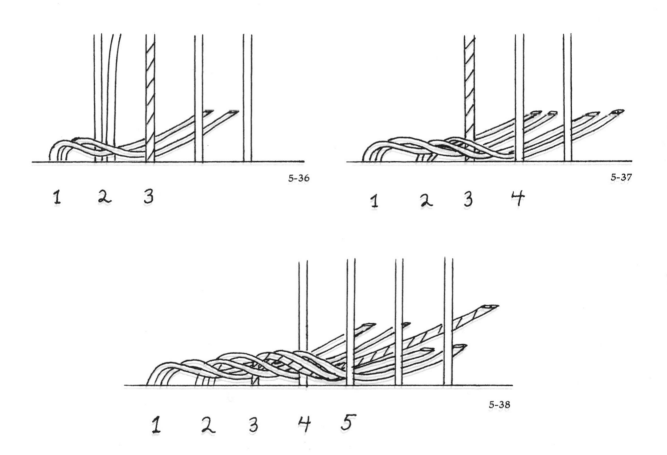

5-36

1 2 3

5-37

1 2 3 4

5-38

1 2 3 4 5

OPEN BORDER I (for fine material)

Step 1. Bend the stakes at about 1″ above the weaving at the top of the basket. Work pattern "back-of-three, over-one, back-of-three, and out." (Fig. 5-39).

Step 2. Work pattern "over-three-and-in" (through curves to inside.) Cut off ends. (Fig. 5-39).

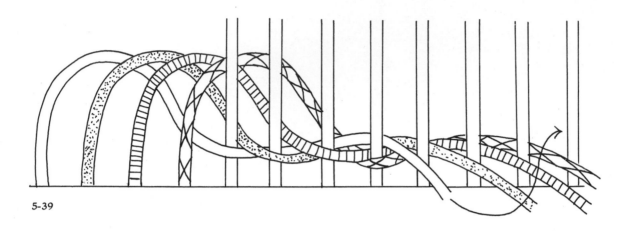

5-39

OPEN BORDER II

Bend stakes down rather sharply about 1½″ above the top of weaving. Work pattern "over-one, under-one, over-one, under-one." The ends of the stakes are lodged behind the next stake. (Fig. 5-40.)

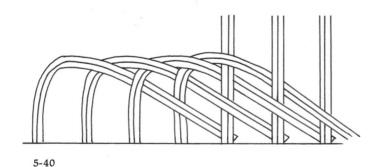

5-40

OPEN BORDER III

Open borders (Fig. 5-41) are used extensively with willow. There is little, if any, side weaving. The stakes are inserted into the base, upsett, taken several inches to the height of the basket, curved over and then woven back toward the base. A foot border secures them. (See Plate 39, page 95.) They are used less successfully with fine material, such as honeysuckle, because the stakes must have a certain rigidity when the borders are completed.

Work pattern "over-two, under-one, over-one, under-one, and out." The dotted lines, emerging between the fifth and sixth sets of stakes, show the threading through of the final standing stakes.

OPEN BORDER IV

The pattern is "over-three, under-two, over-one, under-one and through one-half of the next group and out." (This border is shown in Plate 39; the border in the photograph has been worked to the left.)

MADEIRA BORDERS

Madeira borders are intricate and some of them are difficult to work in willow until a certain amount of experience has been gained. For teaching purposes, the directions are given in successive steps; eventually, you should be able to weave some of them "all of a piece," resorting to the final step of "threading through" only at the end of the round. The borders are less confusing to understand and to work if one concentrates always on the forward movement of the stakes. They are best learned using honeysuckle. When working them in willow, remember to twist the fine willow rods slightly as they are being braided to keep them from breaking. I frequently work these borders while holding the basket entirely under water.

Madeira borders are used most frequently at the foot of the basket where they serve as a stand for it. They can, however, be placed at any level on the sides of the basket (see Plates 40 and 41, pages 96 and 97). Often, the sides are simply woven in openwork Madeira patterns with a closed pattern woven around the base. Baskets made of fine willow or vines are usually woven in randing over long stakes; the stakes are then bordered in a loose scallop design at the top, brought down over the randing on the outside of the basket, and then the foot stand is worked (see Plate 34). Although the stakes in Madeira borders are nearly always multiple (three to six), the illustrations will show only two stakes.

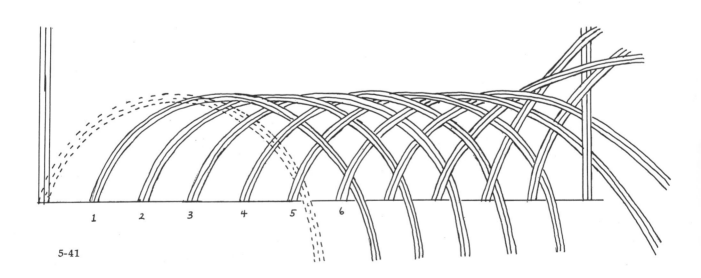

1 2 3 4 5 6

5-41

MADEIRA TOP BORDER I

Take one group of stakes behind the next, out and down. "Back-of-one-and-out." (Fig. 5-42.)

MADEIRA TOP BORDER II

"Over-one-back-of-one-and-out." (Fig. 5-43.)

MADEIRA FOOT BORDER I

This border (Fig. 5-44) is for heavy stiff willow. The basket may be turned upside down or on its side to work the foot.

Step 1. Take a group of stakes, holding them flat, in a close curve behind the next group. Keep the plait close to the edge of the basket by snugging each group and holding the stakes firmly with the left hand until the next group locks them in place. Keep the left hand moving forward as each group is brought around. Thread the last stakes through the pattern.

Step 2. Curve the stakes around for the other side of the plait; take each group "over-one-and-under-the-next" and leave ends protruding at the bottom. Finish round, tighten the plait, if necessary, and trim ends of stakes flush with bottom edge. (If the stakes are started "over-one" instead of being taken "under-one," it can be seen that the ends of the stakes will be concealed beneath the lower curve.)

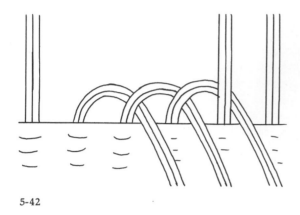

5-42

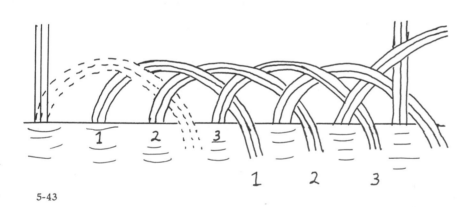

5-43

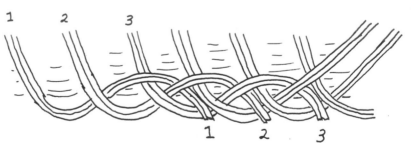

5-44

MADEIRA FOOT BORDER II

This border (Fig. 5-45) is for flexible material.

Step 1. Take the first group of stakes in a loose curve "over-one-under-one" and allow the ends of the stakes to protrude toward the top of the basket. Work all around the basket.

Step 2. Curve Group 1 over Group 4 and thread the ends down toward the bottom of the plait alongside Group 5. Work all around. Adjust the plait and cut off ends.

MADEIRA SIDE BORDER I

This border (Fig. 5-46) is for flexible material.

Step 1. Work Madeira Top Border I (see Fig. 5-42).

Step 2. Draw the top curves closely, then curve Group 1 around and weave it "over-one, under-one, over-one, under-one-and-out toward the top of the basket." Work all around.

Step 3. Curve Group 1 over the next (sixth) group and thread it down through the pattern alongside the seventh group, (dotted lines in the illustration.) Cut off ends.

5-45

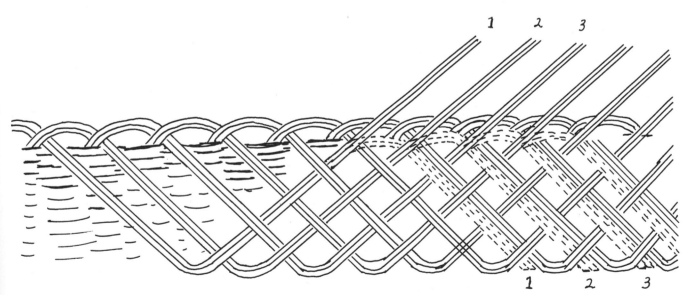

5-46

MADEIRA SIDE BORDER II

This border is for heavy material (see Plate 40, page 96).

Step 1. In a wide curve, work Madeira Top Border II (see Fig. 5-43).

Step 2. Take ends around to the left and weave "over-one, under-one, and out toward the top of the basket." (Fig. 5-47.)

Step 3. Curve ends over the fourth group, under the next ends, over the fifth group and leave ends pointing toward the base (Fig. 5-48).

Step 4. Insert ends under the sixth group and out. Lodge the ends as illustrated. Steps 2 and 3 may be worked at the same time on this border.

HANDLES

ROPED HANDLES

The most common handle found on old wickerwork baskets is the very sturdy roped handle (Fig. 5-49). It is made of medium-sized withes twisted over a thick piece of core wood and, occasionally, over a flat splint.

Select the round core piece before the sides of the basket are woven. Prepare two pieces of willow about 6" long and the same diameter as the ends of the handle core. Insert them into the side weaving where the handles will go. Finish side weaving, working over the temporary stakes as if they were part of the side fabric. Complete basket. (It is not necessary to use the stakes with honeysuckle; the vine will be flexible enough to make an opening for the handle core with an awl.)

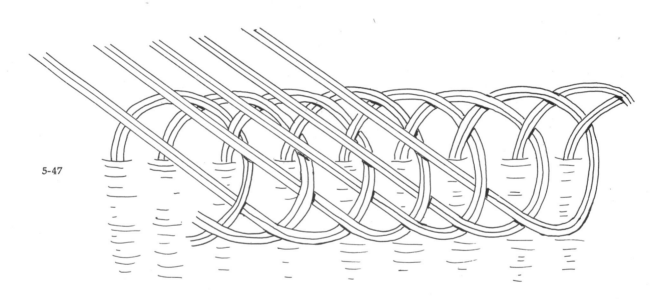

5-47

5-48

Bend handle piece into curve shape. If it is too springy to retain its bowed shape, tie the handle into shape with string and let it dry. Remove the temporary stakes and insert ends of the handle in their stead.

With a well-soaked rod that is twice the length of the handle plus a few inches, insert end through the border into the wale to the left of the handle core. Carry it in front of the handle and begin to wrap it in a spiral to the other side of the handle—five or seven turns, as a rule.

When the other side is reached, loop the end, from the outside toward the inside of the basket, underneath the border. Move the loop an inch or more to the left of the handle; all other loops will rest to the right of this one. Bring the end around in front of the handle and twist the rod back across the core. Since the rod will probably not be long enough to return again, take the end in front of the core, cut it, and insert it into the border beside the beginning end.

Repeat these instructions beginning on the alternate side (Fig. 5-50). Continue adding rods (always at the border) until the core is filled. Keep each rod in the correct groove.

ROPED HANDLE FOR SHORT WILLOW RODS

Insert a handle core into the sides of the basket. Insert two, three, or four rods into the border on one side. Keeping them parallel, spiral them across the handle core to the second side. Insert ends, from the outside, underneath the border and leave them sticking through the weaving temporarily. Insert two or three rods (enough to cover the remaining core) into the border of the second side and wrap them back across the handle. Loop ends, from the outside, under the border, carry them up and around the handle, and down across the inside handle. Tuck ends into the side weaving (Fig. 5-51).

Return to the other side and finish off protruding ends in the same way.

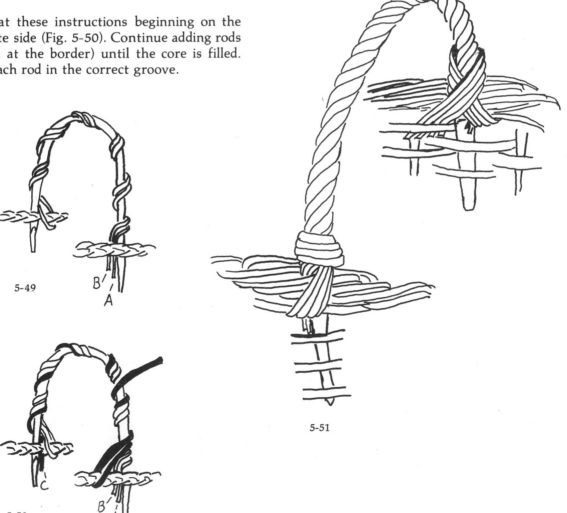

5-49

5-50

5-51

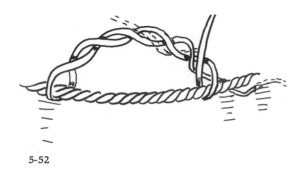

5-52

TWISTED HANDLE WITHOUT A CORE

Loop a thin rod of willow or honeysuckle under the border. Twist the two ends across the handle area and insert them beneath the border from opposite sides. Weave one end away through the weaving and take the other back across (Fig. 5-52), fitting it into the groove. If the piece is long enough, continue to twist back and forth across the handle. The loop goes to the inside of the first loop at each return. The piece is finished off by inserting the end through the border and weaving it away in the side weaving. To add more rods, push ends through border and sew the rod in and out through the proper groove until the handle is filled and tight. The first twists with the initial rod should be about 1" apart. For a thicker handle, leave more space between the twists.

RING HANDLES

For a 2" handle, take an 18" length of fine rod, curve it into a circle and sew the long end in and out around the circle. Repeat a third round, allowing the rod to slip into the groove. Cut off ends neatly (Figs. 5-53, 5-54).

Attach ring handles to basket as shown in Fig. 5-55. This attachment makes a good hinge for a basket lid, also.

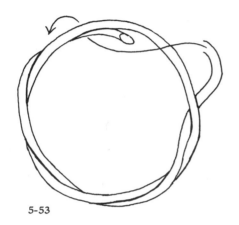

5-53

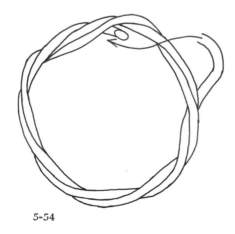

5-54

5-55

BASKET PATTERNS

A ONE-PECK WILLOW BASKET (Plate 33)

Dimensions
Base: 9″
Top: 12″
Height: 6½″

Materials
Nine base spokes (#6) 9″ long
Seventeen side stakes (#6) 20″ long
#4 and #5 willow weavers
Two handle cores ¼″ willow (#8) 11″ long

Base. Make Round Base slath (see Figs. 5-15–5-18), inserting four rods through four. Trim one spoke and add as the extra spoke for a total of seventeen spoke ends. Rand base to 9″ diameter.

Upsett. Single-stake each spoke to a depth of 2″. Work one round of pairing weave before upsetting. Upsett the stakes and tie tops for proper rake of sides.

Sides. Work Three-Rod Wale (see Figs. 5-7–5-9) for 6″.

Border. Work Closed Border I (see Figs. 5-27, 5-28).

Handles. Insert handle core pieces on opposite sides of basket and work Roped Handle (see Figs. 5-49, 5-50) with very fine withes.

33. One-peck willow basket from Virginia.

SCALLOPED HONEYSUCKLE BASKET
(Plate 34, top)

Dimensions
Top: 8"
Overall height: 9½"

Materials
Nine spokes 6¼" long, cut from ¼" butts of willow rods
Thirty-four side stakes (#2) honeysuckle 42" long
Thirty-four by-stakes (#2) honeysuckle 19" long
30–35 yds. (#1 or #2) honeysuckle
Handle: 33" × ⅝" × ⅛" splint

Base. Soak base spokes several hours. Soak honeysuckle twenty minutes. Make Round Base slath (see Figs. 5-15–5-18). Cut one spoke in half and insert it as the odd spoke. There are seventeen spoke ends. Pair around slath twice; spread spokes apart and pair over each spoke for three rounds. Cut off one weaver. Insert the end into the weaving as shown in Fig. 5-12. Rand base until it is 6¼" in diameter.

Upsett. Fold the side stakes in half and double-stake each spoke (4 stakes), inserting stakes to a depth of 1½". Upsett stakes.

Sides. Double a weaver over a group of stakes and work pairing weave for three rounds. Insert by-stakes at outer sides of each group of stakes. Keep stakes in order and flat. Work randing for 2¾". Allow sides to splay outward slightly.

Border. Holding each group of six stakes flat, work Madeira Top Border II (see Fig. 5-43). The top of each scallop stands above the weaving 1½".

Take ends of stakes to the base. Sew a weaver in and out of the weaving at the bottom row of the basket, snugging each group of stakes against the side. Fasten off weaver by weaving ends through the randing.

Soak stakes well. Turn basket on its side, or upside down, and work Madeira Foot Border II (see Fig. 5-45).

Handle. Mark off 10" on each end of handle piece. Taper ends to ¼" width at bottom. Shave the last 6" to a thinness of 1/16" to 1/32".

Bend the handle into an arc and insert ends through one top curve of a scallop (on opposite sides of the basket). Push ends between the lower edge of the basket and the border braid. Adjust top height of handle to 8½" above the center slath.

Take handle ends across the outside of the bottom of the basket, insert ends about 1" from the outside edge of the base and sew the ends into the bottom as shown in Fig. 5-56.

5-56

34. Two Madeira-style baskets. Above: willow basket from Pittsylvania County, Virginia, c. 1890. The basket on the right, made of both willow and honeysuckle c. 1900, from Rockbridge County, Virginia.

AN OAK-ROD WICKERWORK BASKET
(Plates 35 and 36)

This handsome basket contains something of a puzzle: I have been unable to discover the exact tool that was used to shape the evenly planed oak rods. Several elderly basketmakers are familiar with the "oak-rod baskets," but they cannot account for the tool. (This is true, also, of the useful tools employed by European basketmakers in willow. The tools, if they were used at all in the mountains, have long since disappeared.)

The rods appear to have been cut first, into ⅜"-square strips; then they were planed with a circular type of plane. Given the invariable problem of "runouts" in the grain of oak, the blade of the tool would have had to have been set perpendicular to the surface of the wood. The excess surface of the wood would then have been scraped, rather than shaved, off. A hollow, spiral auger would have been a logical tool, but there are no marks on the rods to indicate the use of any kind of spiral cutter. The surfaces are too regular to have been whittled by hand.

Knowing that German cabinetmakers cut furniture dowels by driving short pieces of wood through a piece of steel that had several holes drilled through it, we developed a method that will reproduce the oak rods; however, I am by no means certain that this was the technology in the early nineteenth century. A machine shop will be able to make the tool.

In a 4" × 2" × ¼" piece of cold-rolled steel, have about seven holes drilled along the top of the plate. The holes should range in diameter size from 5/16" to ⅛", at a difference of 1/32" in the diameter of each hole.

Clamp the lower half of the steel plate in a vise. Rive the *green* splints to a square shape, about the width of three annular rings. Whittle the end of a long strip, insert it from the back of the largest hole, and grasp the point with a pair of vise-grip pliers; then, pull the long strip through the hole—hard. Repeat with *each* hole until the proper diameter has been reached. The rods may be sanded. Soak them in water before using, or work them green.

It is vigorous work to reduce an oak pole to 125 smoothly rounded rods: however, the basket can be made with willow or other naturally rounded material.

35. Oak-rod wickerwork basket, c. 1845. These heavy baskets made of carved oak or elm wood are scattered throughout the region of the Shenandoah Valley. Of German origin, they were formerly made in that country of hazel. The evenly planed round rods were cut with a special tool. The technology for making the basket has now been lost in the Applachians.

36. Base of the basket in Plate 35.

Dimensions
Base: 12"
Top: 14"
Height: 10"
Handle from rim to rim: 20"

Materials
Six round oak rods (whittled), ½" in diameter
Forty-eight side stakes, 5/32" diameter, 25" long
Twelve foot-border stakes, 5/32" diameter, 12" long
Handle core: ½" diameter oak rod, 30" long
About 125 weavers, ⅛" diameter, 50" long

Base.   Insert three base rods into three for a Round Base (see Fig. 5-15). Trim weaver to 1/16" thickness and begin pairing weave over base spokes for ¾". Fan out spokes and continue pairing over single spokes for ½". Cut out one weaver. Change to ⅛" weavers and, using chasing technique (see Fig. 5-2), rand until base measures 12" in diameter.

Upsett.   Taper the ends of the forty-eight side stakes and insert them as pairs on each side of the base spokes. Push rods well into weaving toward center of base. Upsett stakes. Tie tops of stakes to proper rake.

Work one round of Four-Rod Wale (Fig. 5-57). Instead of laying in the ends of the wale weavers behind the stakes, *insert* the ends of the four weavers into the weaving of the base, to the left of each of four successive *pairs* of stakes. Bring the long ends around behind the paired stakes and out in front; then, begin Four-Rod Wale.

Sides.   (At a height of 5", insert temporary handle pieces, ⅜" in diameter, on each side of the basket.)

Work 7" of French Slew (see Fig. 5-4) on the sides. (The widest diameter, 15", occurs at the height of 4". After this point, tighten weavers slightly to draw sides into the top diameter of 14".)

Lay in the ends of twenty-four weavers behind successive pairs of spokes and weave the diagonal French slew until the rods run out (about midway up the sides). Level the tops of the rods, slype ends, and lodge them behind successive pairs of stakes. Insert twenty-four more weavers behind stakes and continue French slew. Level weaving and cut off ends of weavers, as before, at the top of the basket.

Work four rounds of Three-Rod Wale (see Figs. 5-7–5-9).

Border.   Cut off the right-hand stake of each pair flush with top of weaving. Work a closed border: "back-of-two, over-two, back-of-one and out" all around. Take each protruding end in front of the next stake and push the end through to the inside of the basket, *under* the border. The border ends will lodge behind the stakes on the inside. Trim ends.

Foot Border.   Turn basket upside down. Insert each of the twelve short stakes through the wale and into the weaving on the sides, alongside one of the pairs of stakes. Insert to a depth of 2".

Take each protruding border stake, to the right, "behind-two, in-front-of-two, behind-one-and-out." Slype ends.

Handle.   Remove temporary handle stakes. Insert handle core ends into weaving. Work a Roped Handle (see Figs. 5-49, 5-50).

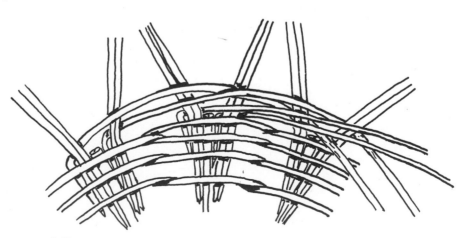

5-57

A DARK BROWN HONEYSUCKLE TRAY
(Plate 37, left)

Dimensions
9½″ × 8″ × 8″ (overall height)

Materials
Seven spokes (#8) 9½″ long
Eleven spokes (#6) 8″ long
Thirty-six stakes (#4) 14″ long
Weavers (#4) wale
Weavers (#3) randing
Handle core: 36″ × ⅜″ × ⅛″

Slath. Make slath 3½″ × 5″ as shown in Fig. 5-21. Rand for 2″ around slath. Single-stake each spoke and work one round of three-rod wale (see Figs. 5-7–5-9).

Upsett. Upsett stakes and work two rounds of three-rod wale.

Sides. Rand two rows. The long ends are raised ½″ by "packing" (see Fig. 5-5). The packing weaver is started around the last stake in the straight section, woven around the curve, across the end section, around the other curve, turning at the first stake on the opposite long side; it is then woven back and forth, as shown in the illustration, until ½″ has been filled in. Weave to the opposite end of the basket and repeat. Work a row of randing all around. Insert two more weavers and work three-rod wale for three rounds.

Border. Work either a Three-Rod Plain Border (see Figs. 5-31–5-33) or Closed Border I (see Figs. 5-27, 5-28).

Handle. Insert handle core splint through weaving at each end of basket and work a roped handle (see Figs. 5-49, 5-50) over the core. Flatten the handle across the top; tie it down to the basket with string to dry into shape.

37. Left: dark brown honeysuckle tray basket, c. 1910. Right: willow market basket. Note similarity to basket in Plate 39 (page 95).

OVAL HONEYSUCKLE BASKET (Plate 31, right)

Dimensions
Base: 9¼" × 5¼" × 5"
Top: 11¼" × 7½"
Overall height: 10"

Materials
Five base spokes (#5) 9¼"
Seven base spokes (#5) 5¼"
One extra spoke (#5) 3"
Seventy-two side stakes (#3 or #4) 12"
Handle core: 33" × ⅜" × ⅛" splint

Base. Make oval slath as shown in Fig. 5-19. Wrap over five long stakes with a small (#2) weaver. Slath is 4¾" long. Insert extra spoke at one end and pair-weave for two rows. Change to randing. Fan out end spokes and weave until base measures 9½" × 5½".

Upsett. Insert pairs of side stakes on each side of end spokes and on *one* side of each side spoke. Work one round of four-rod wale (see page 69) before upsetting. Upsett stakes and work one round of three-rod wale (see Figs. 5-7– 5-9). Tie tops of stakes to achieve proper rake of sides.

Sides. (If willow is used for the basket, weave sides in French slewing.) Using honeysuckle weavers, rand for 1⅜". Work one round of four-rod wale, two rounds of three-rod wale, and one round of four-rod wale. Continue randing for 2". Work four rounds of four-rod wale, taking each rod "over-two, back-of-two and out." This variant pattern will make the wale look like a three-rod wale on both the inside and the outside of the basket.

Border. Cut off left stake of each pair of stakes even with top of weaving.

Work a Three-rod Plain Border (see Figs. 5-31–5-33). Do not cut off ends protruding to outside of basket. Instead, take each end in front of the next stake to the right and insert under the border to the inside of the basket. End rests behind the next stake. Trim, if necessary.

Handle. Insert ends of splint handle core through weaving as shown in the photograph. Trim and thin ends. Adjust top of handle to 10" above center base. Clamp in position at each side of basket. Make a cut through the center of each protruding end of handle at base. Weave both pieces of the ends away through the weaving on bottom of basket.

Work Roped Handle (see Figs. 5-49, 5-50) over handle core. Wedge basket with scrap wood to dry into position.

RECTANGULAR WILLOW MARKET BASKET (Plate 38)

Dimensions
Base: 8" × 10½"
Top: 13" × 17"
Overall height: 16"
Handle from rim to rim: 25"

Materials
Two outside base spokes ½" diameter, 14" long
Five inside base spokes, ⅜" diameter, 14" long
Twenty-six side stakes ⅜" diameter, 26½" long
Four corner posts ½" diameter, 10" long; ¼" round rods and ⅜" wide flat split-willow strips (skeins) for weavers
Handle core: 43" × 1" × ⅛" splint
Two small pegs

Base. Position seven base spokes in a wooden clamp (see Fig. 5-22). Pair a row of willow at the tops of spokes to hold them in position.

Pair-weave the first row at the bottom. Carry weaver around outside rod and begin randing back and forth across spokes. Take an extra turn around outside rods from time to time, to prevent spokes from drawing in toward center. Finish top row with pairing weave. Remove base from clamp and trim spokes flush with weaving.

Upsett. The slyped ends of fourteen stakes, seven on each side, will be inserted through the thick outside base spokes. Make equidistant holes with an awl, beginning and ending about ½" from the ends. Holes are made from the outside, at a slight upward angle. Stick points of stakes in a bar of soap before inserting them through the holes. Insert to depth of 1". (See Fig. 5-24.)

On each narrow end of the base, insert ends of six stakes into weaving, alongside base spokes, to a depth of 2".

Upsett stakes with a slight twist and tie into position at tops of rods.

Sides. With round rods, begin Three-Rod Wale as shown in Fig. 5-25. At each corner, cut a small "shelf" at the bottom inside edge of a corner post, check it for a neat fit, and lock it into position by weaving the wale around it (see Fig. 5-26).

Work two rounds of Three-Rod Wale. Change to split skeins and rand until sides measure 9". Join new weaving skeins by overlapping them through several stakes, as for splint. Add round rods and work two rows of Three-Rod Wale.

Border. Trim corner posts level with top of weaving. Insert four stakes for the border, 12" long, alongside each corner post to a depth of 2".

Work a Four-Rod-Behind-Two Plain Border (see Figs. 5-34, 5-35).

Handle. Open a space beside the fourth stake on the long sides and insert splint handle ends. Slype ends of a 27" willow rod and insert into border on top of splint. Clamp rod to splint at center top.

Bore a ⅛" hole for the pegs through the splint at the lower edge of the wale. Thread the end of a thin willow skein down through the border and insert the end through the hole. Slype end of a willow peg and drive it through the splint, locking the end of the binder skein in place. Trim ends of peg to about ¼" margin. (The pegs hold the handle in place.)

Pull the long end of the skein taut, carry it in front of the splint and begin to wrap across handle. Fig. 5-58 shows the method of joining skeins. At the other side of the handle, make another hole beneath the border, thread end of skein through the splint, peg, and cut off. (In the photograph, the peg is visible at the far inside handle.)

38. Willow market basket, c. 1890. Pocahontas County, West Virginia. The basket is believed to have been made by an itinerant English basketmaker.

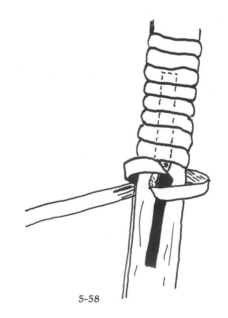

5-58

OPENWORK WILLOW MARKET BASKET
(Plate 39)

Dimensions
Oval base: 16″ × 7½″
Overall height: 14½″

Materials
Three spokes 16″ long, ½″ diameter
Five spokes 7½″ long, ⅜″ diameter
192 willow rods (#5), each 33″ long
Thirty to forty willow rods ¼″ diameter at butts, for base randing
Handle core: 38″ long, ½″ diameter

Slath. Insert three long rods through five short rods. Slath is 10″ long (see Fig. 5-20). This basket does not have an extra stake added. Rand the base by chasing (see Fig. 5-2) two weavers, joining butt to butt and tip to tip. Leave enough room at the outside edges for one round of three-rod wale (see Figs. 5-7–5-9).

39. Willow market basket with Madeira border; brought to Greenbrier County, West Virginia from Maryland in 1880.

Upsett. Slype ends and insert three (33″) stakes on each side of base spokes to a depth of 2″. There will be a total of thirty-two insertions. Work one round of three-rod wale over each group of three stakes; push ends of weavers to bottom of basket and cut off. Upsett the stakes (see page 74).

Sides. Holding each group of three flat, work Open Border IV (see page 81). Hold the tops of the curves at 8½″ above the base. Rewet the stakes often and give the last standing stakes a slight twist as they are being threaded through the pattern.

Border. Level the tops of the scallops. Turn basket on its side, and with the stakes well dampened, work Madeira Foot Border II (see Fig. 5-45).

Handle. Slype ends of the handle core; insert at center sides, and weave ends through curves to the base. Make a roped handle (see Figs. 5-49 and 5-50). Top of handle is 14″ from the center of the base.

WILLOW YARN BASKET (Plate 40)

Dimensions
Top: 18"
Height: 8"

Materials
Eight base spoke (#8) 8⅜" long
Thirty-two stakes (#6) 41" long
Weavers for base and sides (#5)

Base.   Make Round Base slath (see Figs. 5-15–5-18), inserting four spokes through four. Pair weave base.

Upsett.   Double-stake each spoke to a depth of 2". Work one round of Three-Rod Wale (see Figs. 5-7–5-9) before upsetting stakes. Upsett stakes and tie tops to achieve proper rake. Diameter at top of weaving is 15¼".

Sides.   After randing is worked for 1", insert two by-stakes on each side of stakes, for a total of six stakes in each group. Rand until sides measure 5".

Border.   Scallops are 4" above randing. Work Side Border II (see Figs. 5-47 and 5-48).

After border is completed, insert end of a slender rod at the lower edge of the cut-off stakes. Using the photograph as a guide, thread the rod in and out of the plait as far as it will reach. Lodge end underneath a lower curve of the braid. Add another rod, as above, and continue the pattern around the basket.

40. Willow Madeira-style yarn basket, c. 1900. Germany.

HONEYSUCKLE BASKET AFTER FRANCISCO DE ZURBARÁN (Plate 41)

Dimensions
Diameter: 9"
Height: 5½"

Materials
Eleven base spokes ¼" willow
Forty-two stakes honeysuckle (#4) 23" long
Twenty-one stakes honeysuckle (#4) 21" long
Honeysuckle weavers (#2 and #3)
Two handle rings (#5) willow 18" long

Base. Make slath for Round Base (see Figs. 5-15–5-18), inserting five spokes through five. Trim and add extra stake for a total of twenty-one spokes. Rand base to diameter of 9".

Upsett. Insert pairs of long stakes each side of base spokes to a depth of 1½". Work two rounds of Four-Rod Wale (see page 69) before upsetting.

Upsett stakes, change to Three-Rod Wale (see Figs. 5-7–5-9), and work three rounds. (Original willow basket in the painting shows a thick wale at the lower edge of the basket worked over a piece of core.)

Sides. Insert by-stakes through wale to the right of each pair of stakes. Rand until sides measure 5".

Border. Holding stakes flat, work Madeira Top Border I (see Fig. 5-42). Bring stakes down over basket sides about 1¼" before curving stakes upward, toward the right, for Madeira Side Border I (Fig. 5-46). Keep stakes wet while working side border.

Handles. Make two ring handles, 2" in diameter (see Figs. 5-53 and 5-54). Attach to top border with a "twist" of honeysuckle (see Fig. 5-55).

41. Round honeysuckle basket after Francisco de Zurbarán. Contemporary copy.

Coiled Straw

"I haven't seen one of those baskets for years and years . . .
No, the dough didn't stick to the sides because that straw
is hard and slick like the blackberry bark . . . You see, the
straw kept the heat in the bottom to raise the bread."

An 86-year-old Virginia woman

General directions are given here for making
round, oval, and rectangular coiled straw baskets (Plates 18 and 19, pages 24 and 25).

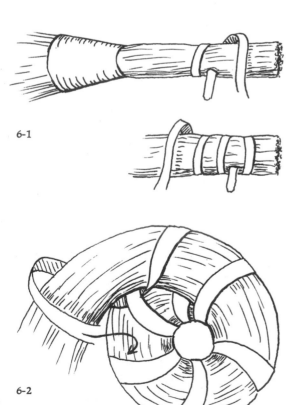

6-1

6-2

ROUND BASES

Fig. 6-1 shows the method of beginning a
coil. (Reduce the size of the coil when starting
a round base.)

After the binder has been anchored in the
straw and several wraps around the end have
been made, curve the coil around on itself and
sew the binder around the first circle, through
the small hole in the center of the circle. The
spiral begins at the second round (Fig. 6-2).

Bring the binder from the back over the top,
open a space with the awl either under the
binder of the lower round (Fig. 6-3) or through
the straw close to the binder (Fig. 6-4). Insert
binder through the opening made by the awl
and tighten it.

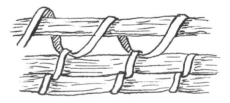

6-3

6-4

As the spiral widens, it will become necessary to work a round with an extra stitch placed between the two stitches on the lower row. Add extra-stitch rounds as often as needed to keep the straw tightly bound (Fig. 6-5).

To turn up the sides, slope the coil gradually for several inches toward the top of the coil.

Fig. 6-6 shows the method of joining new binding strips with a weaver's knot. Pull the knot hard to allow it to bury itself between the coils. (Splint ends may be woven back and forth through different layers of straw in the coil.)

At the top row of the basket, the end of the coil should be thinned to taper it for several inches. This will permit the end of the spiral to be "killed" into the round beneath it. Border the top row with close binding or with a criss-cross lashing (see Plate 19, page 25).

Handles can be formed at the top row by pulling a section of the coil out from the basket and wrapping it separately for a few inches. Rejoin it to the main coil and continue as before.

Splint handles are made for coiled baskets by shaping them into a curve and wrapping their ends in with the coiling. Add splint handles one or two rows below the top row.

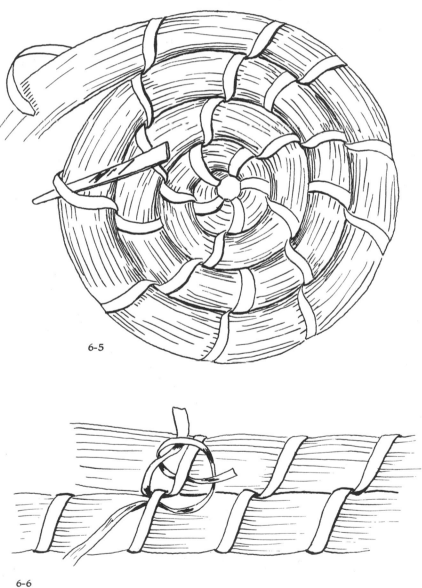

6-5

6-6

OVAL BASES

Fig. 6-7 illustrates the beginning of a coil for an oval basket. Oval baskets usually have straight sides.

6-7

RECTANGULAR BASES

The diagram in Fig. 6-8 shows the arrangement of the coil for a rectangular bottom. As the base of the basket enlarges, take an extra stitch or two in the four corners.

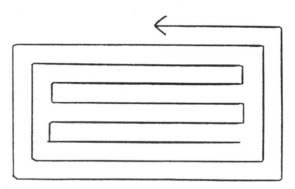

6-8

LIDS

To fit a lid to a coiled basket, make lid large enough to cover the top. Turn lid over and sew an extra coil on the bottom of it. The extra coil should fit down inside the top of the basket to hold the lid in place. Slip the ends of a small splint handle through several binders at the center top.

Hearth Brooms

"Brooms is a lot of fun to make, but now, if you want to know the truth about it, the tourists likes 'em and all, but I'd a heap rather have one from the store to *use* ... The wire holds 'em together better."

A broom maker from Virginia

There are several styles of mountain broom, the oldest being the "birch besom," made of seasoned birch twigs. (Fig. 7-1).

Twigs and small branches were cut in late autumn, stacked in bundles under a shed, and air dried for two or three months. Handles for the brooms were whittled from hickory, ash, and oak and pointed on one end.

The broom maker gathered a handful of coarse twigs for the core of the broom head and surrounded this with smaller, more delicate "sweeps" (twigs). Before binding, the head measured 5" or 6" in diameter. The top of the broom was wrapped with two bands of tightly pulled splint about 3" apart. The top and bottom were then trimmed with an axe and the pointed end of the handle driven into the center of the core and nailed in two places, just below the splint bands, to keep the handle from twisting out of the broom.

My grandfather and I once watched an interesting contest involving a besom broom. The floor of an old store building was being given its annual oiling. Oil had been sloshed all over the floor and spread about with mops. After the wood had absorbed all of the oil it was minded to, the task of cleaning up the residue was left to several men with sacks of sawdust and pushbrooms. One of the men had a large besom broom with him. A friendly wager concerning the merits of the two styles of broom was laid on. A more rigorous test for a broom could hardly be devised than the Augean task of sweeping up oil-saturated sawdust plus a year's accumulation of dust and mud oozing from old floorboards. The besom lost the contest, as I remember, but the men were impressed with its performance. I remember, too, that the birch broom was noisy.

Broom corn, a variety of sorghum, is the usual material for brooms nowadays (Fig. 7-2).

7-1

7-2

Broom-corn seeds are available from some seed companies, and also, from a careful culling of *new* brooms standing in racks in grocery stores. With the permission of your grocer, look into the core area of several brooms. A few seeds will often be seen clinging to the straws. The seed grows exactly like corn. (If only three or four plants can be grown to maturity, there will be enough seed to plant at least a quarter of an acre the following year!)

When the plant has matured in August, bend down the top stalk containing the straws and seed heads; snap it off. Dry the green straw with its stalk in a dry area for a month or more. The seeds are most easily removed (when thoroughly dry) by drawing the straws under the teeth of a handsaw held against a flat surface.

MAKING A BROOM

Select straws for the broom and soften them in tepid water for twenty minutes.

Prepare several long, thin strips of splint, or bark, for the binding.

Bundle the stalks together at the junction of the straws and the stalks. Insert the end of a splint through the stalks, roll the bundle over on the splint one and a half times, and pull the splint hard. It must be tight. Proceed to wrap spirally up the stalks, keeping the binder taut (Fig. 7-3).

Near the top, clamp the binder to the stalks while the handle is being formed.

The handle is made from the ends of the stalks. Allow one or two outside stalks to pro-

trude 4" above the others. Cut off the remaining stalks with an even cut. Curve the handle around. Abut the cut ends against the stalks and place the protruding stalk flat against the straight stalks (Fig. 7-4). Release the clamp and continue wrapping, catching in the handle stalk (Fig. 7-5). Pull binding close. Wrap around the handle section, take one full turn around the end, and return, making an X-lashing for one or two turns. Insert the end of the binder through the stalks, tighten and cut off the end (Fig. 7-6).

Another style of hearth broom has a spirally carved handle of hardwood (Fig. 7-7). The handle is attractive in walnut. Mark pattern for the spiral on a piece of square stock. Use a rasp, chisels, and a penknife to cut the grooves.

Slype the ends of the stalks and layer them around the end of the handle. Slip the end of the binder beneath several stalks and tack it to the handle; roll the broom over a time or two on the binder, step on the end of the binder, and, using as much body weight as possible, tighten the binder; clamp it. The head of the broom is woven in randing for 2½" or 3". Lift up even groups of straws or stalks, ease the weaver through the first round, then release the clamp and pull the weaver through. Retighten the weaver. Work the second row. Pack the rows against each other tightly.

At the end of weaving the cuff, the weaver may be tacked to the end of the handle, or bound around the lower edge of the weaving, pulled tautly, and then nailed, through the straw, to the handle end.

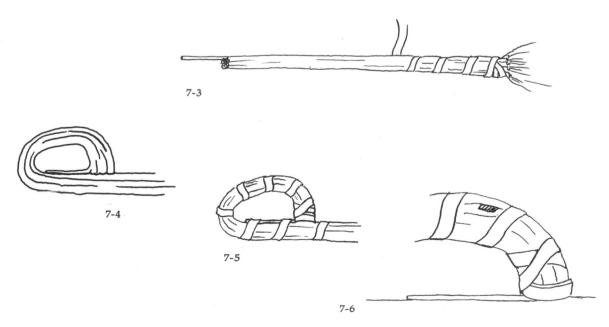

7-3

7-4

7-5

7-6

SEWING THE STRAW

Loop a long, doubled piece of tightly twisted cord, or a thin splint, around an outside group of straws; push ends through loop (Fig. 7-8). Tighten knot and wrap cords completely around broom, inserting ends up through straw beside first knot (Fig. 7-9). Sew cords diagonally over wrapping, up and down through straw, catching binder in a stitch on the other side (Fig. 7-10). Sew back across broom, making an X-lashing (Fig. 7-11). Tie off ends of cord with a couple of half-hitch knots wrapped around the beginning loop.

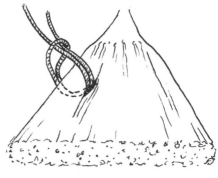

7-8

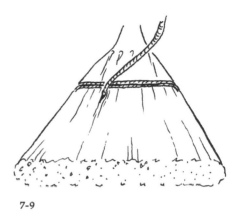

7-9

7-7

7-10

7-11

Dyestuffs

"I think they didn't dye or paint the baskets for the same reason that they didn't paint their houses—we were all too tired. We had to work hard just to eat and a basket was just something plain, something you *used*, like a hoe or an axe handle ... just plain wood. Goodness me! Who had time to pretty them up?"

A West Virginia woman

SPLINTS

It is imperative that any wood to be dyed in a water bath be trimmed and smoothly planed, even sanded, before it is submitted to the soaking. Water will raise the grain of the wood, and the finished basket will have a coarse look to it unless steps are taken to prevent it.

I have seen, in the course of my travels, two or three dyed baskets that were perfectly finished. This means that the splints, to begin with, were taken from a superior tree. After cutting, they were planed to a satin smoothness, soaked in plain water for a couple of hours, dried, and then planed or scraped again to remove the fibers raised by the water. Only then were they given to the dyebath. The splints were probably lightly scraped again after the dyebath. The basketmakers who made such baskets as these (see Plate 29) were obviously acquainted with the techniques of fine finishing practiced by good cabinetmakers. (Baskets may be soaked in a dyebath after they have been completed, but this is not the recommended procedure.)

Some craftsmen worry too much about the "new" look of a freshly made basket. The baskets darken rather quickly as they age indoors, but if the process *must* be hurried along, paint the splints with full-strength ammonia. Ammonia will not raise the grain of the wood so much as water. Tea or coffee will stain splints, also.

The traditional dyes for splint baskets are made from the products of two trees—black walnut and white oak. The dyes are used without mordants. (Bloodroot [*Sanguinaria canadensis*] was used by Indian dyers to stain splints a red-orange. It is a hazard to continue to use the roots of this little wildflower: not only is the plant endangered thereby, but the dye is definitely fugitive.)

DARK BROWN

Black Walnut (*Juglans nigra*) nut hulls or bark. If time allows, fill a five-gallon paint can with walnuts in the autumn and set the can in the open to collect rainwater and to steep throughout the winter. Strain off the saturated dye into plastic milk jugs about every two months. The nuts will continue to give off a rich dye for eighteen months or longer. This stain is very permanent. The dyer is advised to wear rubber gloves and old clothing when working near it.

The material to be dyed is allowed to steep in a tub or kettle with the dye for about a week.

To extract the color and to dye splints (or vines) in the same operation, layer the splints in a tub with about fifteen handfuls of bark, or three gallons of nuts with hulls left on, cover with water and simmer for twelve hours. Allow it to steep for another twelve hours. Rinse until water runs clear after dyeing.

SILVER GRAY

White oak (*Quercus alba***) bark.** Collect all of the bark of the log from which splints have been taken. Place it in a tub, cover with water, and allow it to steep for four days. Strain off the dye. Soak splints in the dyebath for another four days.

Trees from a clay soil containing a high percentage of alum will give off a bronze-gray color, rather than the desired purple-silver gray.

WILLOW

Willow is normally stained its buff-tan color by the tannin released from the bark during its processing. Spring-cut willow, peeled when the sap is up in the withes, is white.

HONEYSUCKLE

Honeysuckle is the material with the most scope for dyeing with colors other than wood tones. Use water-based colors.

One may be extravagantly experimental with honeysuckle. It absorbs all dye readily: commercial cloth dyes found in grocery stores, the full range of vegetable dyes used with proper mordants, artists' acrylic colors, and aniline stains soluble in alcohol or water. (Some aniline reds and greens are fugitive in sunlight.)

Vegetable dyes are soft, or *subtle*, in their coloring. By this is meant that the hues contain a mixture of colors of varying reflected lightwaves. Cloth dyed with vegetable dyes is noted for its capacity to blend well with many other colors.

Commercial aniline dyes, easier to use than vegetable dyes, often fail in the hands of home dyers because a single intense color is used alone. If the purpose is to approximate a color produced by a vegetable dye, the dyer should neutralize, or "gray" a commercial dye in one of two ways. Using a color wheel as a guide, add a small amount of the *complementary* color to the dye color, or better yet, add a very small amount of as many as three or four of the *related* tertiary colors to the dye color.

A favorite trick of cabinetmakers in blending colors for stains is to neutralize their colors by the addition of one of the "earth colors" (umbers, siennas, yellow ochre, lampblack) containing either the complement or a related color.

FINISHES

The question of surface finishing with oil or varnishes is often raised. The answer is: *no!* This is not a mere matter of taste; it is important to the survival of the material that the pores of the thin wood should remain open and be allowed to contract and expand with changes in humidity. It should be pointed out that linseed-oil finishes oxidize into "varnishes" and that the oil attracts dust and grime. The only oil that looks right on the handles of splint baskets is that from the human hand, through years of use.

A basket is already rich in texture. A well-proportioned basket is sufficiently enhanced by the tactile beauty of the raw wood if the splints are evenly cut and smoothly polished by a tool in the hands of a patient craftsman.

Novelty baskets are another matter. They are not made for the ages and one may feel free to finish them with thinned coats of varnish, lacquer, or paint. They may even be gilded with silver- or gold leaf.

Cleaning and Conservation of Old Baskets

"My mother used to leave our baskets out in the snow every once in a while; she said snow was good to keep the baskets limber."

A Virginia schoolteacher

Moisture *within* the cells of wood never completely dries; moisture *between* the cells is constantly changing according to the moisture content of the atmosphere. Subjecting wood to sudden changes of humidity, such as plunging an extremely brittle old basket into a tub of hot water, is likely to result in some cracking. Bring the atmospheric moisture content up (or down) slowly. Let an old basket sit in a shower room for two or three weeks, or steam it over boiling water twice a day for several days before submitting it to a water bath or *gentle* spraying in order to clean it.

Begin a cleaning operation by brushing the basket with a *soft* paint brush. Loosen dirt in the interstices with the brush, then blow it out. The next operation is steaming. Often, surface dirt can be removed entirely after a light steaming.

If cleaning must progress to washing, use soft water and a *small* amount of sudsing ammonia. Wet the basket just enough to dampen the surface and brush lightly with a soft brush. Rinse the basket by spraying water on it. Allow it to dry slowly in a shady spot. If the basket has lost some of its original shape, brace it with pieces of scrap wood while it is drying.

Willow and honeysuckle are cleaned in the same way, and wheat-straw baskets may be cleaned with a stronger solution of ammonia and water.

Baskets should be cleaned once a year, and, if they are stored in overheated, dry rooms, they should be "moisturized" in the shower room for a couple of weeks in midwinter.

Unfortunately, it is not uncommon to find a fine old splint basket that has been "skinned" by some energetic dealer. The basket has been roughly submerged in a tub of hot water and scrubbed with strong soap and a coarse scrub brush. Examination of the basket reveals withered-looking splints, raised grain fibers on the handle, and broken splints. Dirt and the original patina can be detected deep in the interstices, but the high spots of the surface will look almost bleached.

The restoration of such a basket as an "antique" is never completely successful; however, it can be restored to a useful life and attractiveness.

After new splints have been cut and added to the basket to replace damaged splints, sand the handle and as much of the surface of each splint as can be reached with a fine #220 grit sandpaper. The handle may be scraped with a piece of glass and then polished by rubbing it with a smooth piece of hardwood.

After smoothing as much of the surface of the basket as it is possible to do, vacuum the basket to remove the dust.

Dissolve one teaspoon of refined asphaltum in one cup of mineral spirits. (This is the only instance in which I use oil on a basket—and it is a sticky mixture at that.) Wipe the amber stain on the basket splints and the handle and rub it into the wood. The oil vehicle will carry the asphaltum into some of the crevices in the wood and then it will evaporate. Wipe the basket daily for two or three days with a clean cloth, or until all traces of the asphaltum have disappeared from the top surface of the wood. This treatment will restore some of the look of age and patina to the basket, particularly as the asphaltum collects dust and that, in turn, is used as color. By the end of a year, when the basket is ready for its annual cleaning, the basket will begin to resemble its former state before its somewhat violent ablution. The new splints may be stained to match the old, but if one is striving for historical authenticity, this is not necessary. Splint baskets were frequently patched by their owners throughout the years.

Willow and honeysuckle baskets are easily repaired. Soak the baskets for two or three days to render them pliable. Cut out damaged rods and insert new ones alongside the old. Use an awl to open up spaces in borders for inserting new ends. Try to match colors on these materials before working them into place. Artists' acrylic colors are useful for this purpose.

Advice to Collectors

"I wouldn't part with that basket for anything in the world! Everytime I look at it, I can just see my grandmother comin' over the hill at home to see us with that old basket over her arm. She always had it filled to the top with preserves, or homemade bread, or something she'd made for us.

A West Virginia woman

Old baskets for sale today are more likely to be found in the foothills surrounding the mountains than in the mountains. The baskets were purchased in the nineteenth century by denizens of the piedmont areas who went to vacation at the many spas, or who had summer homes in the cool mountains. These baskets came into urban homes where they led serviceable, but relative easy, lives. This is why they are often in mint condition. Prices for old baskets vary considerably with the region. One indication of their increasing value is that they have been moving steadily away from flea market sales and into antique shops.

For several years, it has been a rare occasion when new splint baskets were offered for sale. A basket that cost two and a half dollars twenty years ago now costs twenty dollars, and it is doubtful whether the basketmaker is adequately compensated for his or her labor at that price.

Sources of Supply

Mr. Elvin D. Frame, Supervisor of Forest
  Products
  Virginia Division of Forestry
  Charlottesville, Virginia 22903 (for access to
  white-oak logs)

Williams Electric Co., Inc.
  2108 School Lane
  Lynchburg, Virginia 24501 (for handmade
  craft tools)

Peerless Rattan and Reed Mfg. Co., Inc.
  97 Washington Street
  New York, New York 10006 (for rattan cane
  and reed and hand-rived white-ash splints)

The H. H. Perkins Company
  10 South Bradley Road
  Woodbridge, Connecticut 06525 (for rattan
  cane and reed and white-oak splints)

SUBSTITUTE MATERIALS

In this book, rattan reed may be substituted
for willow and vine materials used in wickerwork. American reed sizes are given in parentheses in the directions.

American Number	Diameter in Inches	Millimeter Size
0	1/64	1.25
1	1/32	1.5
2	1/16	1.75
3	3/32	2.25
4	7/64	2.75
5	1/8	3.25
6	5/32	4
7	3/16	4.75
8	1/4	6
10	10/32	8
12	3/8	10

Machine-cut ash or oak splints are sometimes available from specialty craft supply
houses. Thicker handles and rims will still have
to be made from heavier stock. If machine-cut
splints are used, care must be taken to determine the *outside* surface of the splint. If a bend
is made from the inside surface of the splint
toward the outside, the strips will splinter.
The smoother side of the splint should be facing to the outside of the basket.

Bibliography

(Recommended books for basketmaking are marked with an asterisk.)

Ashley, Gertrude P., and Ashley, Mildred. *Raffia Basketry as a Fine Art*. Deerfield: By the Authors, 1915.

Beecher, Catherine E. *A Treatise on Domestic Economy*. Boston: Marsh, Capen, Lyon and Webb, 1841.

"Began Basketmaking at Age of 12." *Amherst (Va.) New Era-Progress*. 12 July 1973, p. 9.

Blanchard, Mary M. *The Basketry Book*. New York: C. Scribner's Sons, 1914.

Blandford, Percy W. *Country Craft Tools*. New York: Funk and Wagnalls, 1976.

Bobart, H. H. *Basketwork Through the Ages*. London: Oxford University Press, 1936.

Bronson, J. and R. *The Domestic Manufacturer's Assistant and Family Directory in the Arts of Weaving and Dyeing*. Utica, New York: W. Williams, 1817.

Caldwell, John Edwards. *A Tour Through Part of Virginia in the Summer of 1808 and also Some Account of the Islands in the Atlantic Ocean Known by the Name of The Azores*. Belfast: Smyth and Lyons, 1810. Reprint edition edited by Wm. M. E. Rachal, Richmond: The Dietz Press, Inc., 1951.

Christopher, F. J. *Basketry*. London: W. and G. Foyle, 1951.

Cock, Micajah R. *The American Poultry Book*. New York: Harper and Brothers, 1844.

Cornelius, Mary Hooker. *The Young Housekeeper's Friend*, Rev. ed. Boston: Taggart and Thompson, 1864.

The Cultivator. "The Osier Willow." (March 1835) p. 37.

Cummings, Abbott Lowell, ed. *Rural Household Inventories*. Boston: The Society for the Preservation of New England Antiquities, 1964.

Deane, Samuel. *The New England Farmer or Georgical Dictionary*. Worcester, Massachusetts: Isiah Thomas, 1797.

Derry, Thomas K. *A Short History of Technology from the Earliest Times to A. D. 1900*. New York: Oxford University Press, 1961.

Drowne, William. *Compendium of Agriculture*. Providence: Field and Maxey, 1824.

*Eaton, Allen H. *Handicrafts of the Southern Highlands*. New York: The Russell Sage Foundation, 1937.

Firth, Annie. *Cane Basket Work*. London: L. Upcott Gill, 1901.

Forbes, Robert James. *Studies in Ancient Technology*. Vol. IV. Leiden: E. J. Brill, 1964.

Gill, Anna A. *Practical Basketry*. Philadelphia: D. McKay, 1916.

Goodrich, Frances L. *Mountain Homespun*. New Haven: Yale University Press, 1931.

Gould, Mary Earle. *Early American Wooden Ware*. Springfield, Massachusetts: Pond-Ekberg Co., 1948.

Graves, Robert. *White Goddess*. New York: Farrar, Straus, & Giroux, 1966.

Green, Sir J. L. *The Rural Industries of England*. London: E. Marlborough and Co., 1895.

*Harvey, Virginia I. *The Techniques of Basketry*. New York: Van Nostrand Reinhold Co., 1974.

Hopf, Carol J. "Basketware of the Northeast: A Survey of the Types of Basketware Used on the Farm from the Colonial Period to 1860." Thesis, Cooperstown Graduate Program, State University of New York College at Oneonta, 1965.

James, George Wharton. *Indian Basketry*. New York: H. Malkan, 1902.

*Jenkins, J. Geraint. *Traditional Country Craftsmen*. New York: Frederick A. Praeger, 1966.

*Knock, A. G. *Willow Basket-work*. 6th ed. Leicester: The Dryad Press, 1958.

*Krochmal, Arnold and Connie. *The Complete Illustrated Book of Dyes from Natural Sources*. Garden City, New York: Doubleday and Co., 1974.

Laird, Catherine C. "Basketry Notes." Mimeographed. Elkins, West Virginia: 1967 (?).

Lang, Mrs. Edwin. *Basketry Weaving and Design*. New York, Charles Scribner's Sons, 1925.

Lassaigne, Jacques. *Spanish Painting*. Vol. 2. New York: Skira, 1952.

Lichten, Frances. *Folk Art of Rural Pennsylvania*. New York: Charles Scribner's Sons, 1946.

Manners, J. E. *Country Crafts Today*. Newton Abbot, England: David and Charles, 1974.

Morton, Oren F. *A History of Rockbridge County*. Staunton, Virginia: The McClure Co., 1920.

*Okey, Thomas. *An Introduction to the Art of Basket-Making*. London: Pittman and Sons, 1912.

O'Neil, Isabel. *Art of the Painted Finish for Furniture and Decoration*. William Morrow and Co., 1971.

Peters, Harry T. *Currier and Ives, Printmakers to the American People*. New York: Doubleday and Co., 1942.

Pittaway, Andy and Scofield, Bernard. *Traditional English Country Crafts*. New York: Random House, Pantheon Books, 1975.

Rossbach, Ed. *Baskets as Textile Art*. New York: Van Nostrand Reinhold Co., 1973.

Sandford, Lettice. *Strawwork and Corn Dollies*. New York: The Viking Press, 1974.

*Schneider, Richard C. *Crafts of the North American Indians*. New York: Van Nostrand Reinhold Co., 1974.

Singer, Charles Joseph. *A History of Technology*. Oxford: Clarendon Press, 1954–58.

Strausbaugh, P. D. and Core, Earl L. *Flora of West Virginia*. 2nd ed. Morgantown: West Virginia University Bulletin, 1971.

Teleki, Gloria Roth. *The Baskets of Rural America*. New York: E. P. Dutton & Co., 1975.

*Tod, Osma Gallinger. *Earth Basketry*. New York: Crown Publishers, Bonanza Books, 1972.

White, Iris Bryson. *Sussex Crafts*. Bourne End, England: Spurbooks, 1974.

White, Mary. *How to Make Baskets*. New York: Doubleday, Page and Co., 1901.

———. *More Baskets and How to Make Them*. New York: Doubleday, Page and Co., 1903.

*Wigginton, Eliot, ed. *The Foxfire Book*. New York: Doubleday and Co., Anchor Books, 1972.

*Wright, Dorothy. *Baskets and Basketry*. Newton Abbot, England: David and Charles, 1974.

Wymer, Norman. *English Country Crafts*. London: Batsford, 1946.

Index